Be Still, Be Silent

Also by John Mann

Lent with Saint John's Gospel, 2014.

Journeying to the Light, 2023.

Christ's Seven Words from the Cross, 2024.

Moments of Love: An eight-day retreat with the Song of Songs, 2025.

Be Still, Be Silent

*Reflections on the poetry
of David Scott*

John Mann

CANTERBURY
PRESS

© John Mann 2025

Published in 2025 by Canterbury Press

Editorial office
3rd Floor, Invicta House,
110 Golden Lane,
London EC1Y 0TG, UK
www.canterburypress.co.uk

Canterbury Press is an imprint of Hymns Ancient & Modern Ltd
(a registered charity)

Hymns Ancient & Modern® is a registered trademark of
Hymns Ancient & Modern Ltd
13A Hellesdon Park Road, Norwich,
Norfolk NR6 5DR, UK

All rights reserved. No part of this publication may be reproduced,
stored in a retrieval system, or transmitted,
in any form or by any means, electronic, mechanical,
photocopying or otherwise, without the prior permission of
the publisher, Canterbury Press.

John Mann has asserted his right under the Copyright, Designs and
Patents Act 1988 to be identified as the Author of this Work

Scripture quotations are from New Revised Standard Version Bible:
Anglicized Edition, copyright © 1989, 1995 National Council of the
Churches of Christ in the United States of America. Used by permission.
All rights reserved worldwide.

British Library Cataloguing in Publication data

A catalogue record for this book is available
from the British Library

ISBN: 978-1-78622-675-4

EU GPSR Authorised Representative
LOGOS EUROPE, 9 rue Nicolas Poussin, 17000, LA ROCHELLE, France
E-mail: Contact@logoseurope.eu

Typeset by Regent Typesetting
Printed and bound by
CPI Group (UK) Ltd

Contents

Tribute to 'Pietà' by Mark Oakley   vii
Foreword by Malcolm Guite   ix
Acknowledgements   xii
Introduction   xiii

1 Annunciation   1
2 Nativity   17
3 Crucifixion   33
4 Resurrection   51

Afterword   61
Epilogue: The first David Scott Lecture
given by Mark Oakley   73
Bibliography   87
David Scott's published works listed chronologically   88
Endnotes   89
Index of poems   95

Pietà

by Mark Oakley

Pietà

What worth piety now?
How much it's lost its thrust,
its endless duty, its heave, its thuds.
So I came a long way round to find
the plangent, aching sorrow,
that only death can handle wisely.
As Mary held her baby in her arms;
so now, again, the mother holds the son;
in death, and wonder, both.[1]

'Pietà' is probably David Scott's last poem. He wrote it in response to Peter Ball's sculpture in Winchester Cathedral of Mary holding the lifeless body of her son in her arms. In many ways it poignantly encapsulates David's poetic work. Assured with reticence, and patient with life's filtered light, it takes us to the border crossing between a life's pain and its distillation. Like much of his work, there is a modesty of tone held in place by an unadorned reverence for life which, because of its holy and mysterious source, is offered to us, against many odds, as being worthy of our trust and love. In David's poems life's immensities are intimate and its intimacies are immense.

The opening question of the poem does not seek to shock or dramatize. It emerges from a transparency that can do nothing else than ask the honest question in our company. Have piety's 'duty' and 'thrust' given way to an attentiveness or orientation towards the more universal 'aching sorrow' that the Pietà witnesses to so starkly? One senses that the passing of devout distractions and ritualized ways of thinking within has led to a renewed, attentive sense of 'wonder', with both senses of that word in full play. As this poem turns the page to a lifetime's work, another end that must inevitably come falls into view – and with the same disconcerted trust of repair and homecoming.

The Very Revd Mark Oakley
Dean of Southwark

Foreword

by Malcolm Guite

I am delighted to write the Foreword to this book, for I am one of the many who not only cherish David Scott's poetry, but also owe him a debt of gratitude for the way he mediated faith, not only through his nurturing poetic imagination but also through his personal presence, his way of living and being in the world.

I first met him during my troubled teenage years, when he became the only chaplain at my school to take an interest in and care for the small group of boys cooped up in a great day school's neglected boarding house.

At the time, I was fiercely atheist and took the opportunity of my encounters with him to try and trounce his faith. I had become obsessed with Samuel Beckett, and I remember reciting bits of Beckett at him, as though the mere existence of *Waiting for Godot* was sufficient to finish Christianity for ever.

His response was both unexpected and disarming. 'Ah, Malcolm,' he said. 'I'm so glad you've discovered Beckett, that Desert Father of the High Modernists.' Of course, I didn't know what a Desert Father was and had to ask. He put the right books in my hands, and it was a strangely moving experience to read the lives and sayings of the fathers, as though these ragged figures shared a stage with Estragon and Vladimir.

I came back for more, and David and I became good friends. He let slip that, as well as being a chaplain, he was that most mysterious of things – a poet. I even took the risk of telling him that was what I wanted to be too. He could not have been more gracious and encouraging to my fledgling literary ambition.

We stayed in touch after I left school, and he showed me what I most wanted to know: that Christianity was a living faith, and that poetry and priesthood were real vocations. He showed me, both in his life and his poetry, how one might live within the poetic tradition and also within the two great poems of liturgy and scripture; and yet still be open to all the nuances and complexities, the doubts and perturbations of contemporary life.

We also shared, it turned out, a deep and formative interest, amounting to veneration, in Lancelot Andrewes, and he gave me the beautiful translations he made of Andrewes's private prayers, which were renewed in David's deft re-imagining as contemporary poems.

Now I open again the pages of my worn copy of *Playing for England*, the book that also first inspired John Mann, whose new book you have in your hands. Poem after poem from that collection speaks to me in David's gentle searching voice. As I vest for a service, his little poem 'The Surplice' comes back to me. I hear him say:

> For me it is my only finery, by law
> decent and comely; a vestry friend
> put on often in dread; given away
> to old deft fingers to mend.[2]

And, on funeral days, I remember his glimpse of the surplice

> chucked on the back seat of the car
> with the purple stole and the shopping.

In some ways, his poetry has been like that for me: both a beautiful, time-honoured clothing, and also a companion in the midst of the everyday. What he says of the surplice in the last lines of that poem also stands for and summons the two traditions, spiritual and poetic, that his life and poetry have helped me to inhabit:

FOREWORD

We have put these garments on for centuries.
They persist. We wither and crease inside them.

I was thrilled therefore to learn that John Mann was writing a book on David Scott's poetry. I think the poet himself would thoroughly approve of the approach this book takes. It is the same approach that John Donne took in his sonnet sequence *La Corona*: to begin with the Annunciation and take us through from there, through the Nativity and the Crucifixion to the Resurrection. For in that sequence of mysteries we journey through the heart of the Christian Mystery itself, a mystery before which cold prose fails and falls silent, but poetry comes into its own.

John Mann handles the poetry deftly and skilfully, opening it out to us, inviting us into the poem, and the poem into us. Never imposing an interpretation narrowly, or foreclosing on all the possibilities of meaning, but giving us just the information and insights we need to lift the veil a little and see beneath the surface.

The best literary criticism is the kind that turns and returns you to the text itself with new enthusiasm and insight, and that is the kind of writing you have here. My hope is that this book will send many readers back to the poems themselves and be part of a recovery and revival of interest in a poet whose reputation and place in the literary and spiritual cannon can only increase with the passing years. It is many times too true that it is only after a poet's death, after their life's work is complete, that we begin to see them in their true proportions and learn the real value of all they have left for us. *Be Still, Be Silent* will, I think, be the beginning of that deeper valuation of the work of David Scott.

The Revd Dr A Malcolm Guite
Fellow of Girton College, Cambridge

Acknowledgements

This book has only been possible with the help of a number of people through the stages of writing, submission, design, permissions and final production – particularly my wife Helen, for all she says and does to ensure that both the joy and discipline of writing continue in equal measure. I would also like to thank especially Miggy, whose kindness, understanding, questions, corrections, observations, support and encouragement have been essential. To Malcolm Guite for tending the initial seed of an idea, and who so willingly offered to write the Foreword, I am truly grateful. To Mark Oakley for his tribute to probably David's last poem, 'Pietà', and allowing the text of his 2017 David Scott Lecture to be included, and for thereby placing in context a reflection on one poet within the capacity of poetry to affect us, again I am deeply thankful. I would like to thank also the staff at Canterbury Press, especially Christine Smith and Rachel Geddes, for their advice and guidance, and to all who have shown patience and help, particularly Suzanne Fairless-Aitken, rights and permissions officer at Bloodaxe Books.

Finally, I add recognition of the importance to this publication of all the quotations, whether requiring actual permission or not, with personal thanks:

Acknowledgement for the reproduction of David's poetry:
David Scott, *Beyond the Drift: New & Selected Poems*,
Bloodaxe Books, 2014.
Reproduced with permission of Bloodaxe Books.
www.bloodaxebooks.com
@bloodaxebooks (twitter/facebook) #bloodaxebooks

Introduction

It was in 1993 or 1994 that I bought a slim poetry collection entitled, *Playing for England*. I was discovering poetry and reading some poets who were writing at the time. I loved every one of David's poems in this book, reading and rereading, quoting some in sermons and more especially when leading retreats. I wanted to follow the thread that ran through the words to the faith that lay within his fertile and appealing personality. With him, I lifted a stone and glanced through a window, felt the breeze and above all was still and silent, for he knew the God I sought, and I was comfortable in his presence.

When David died in October 2022, after being ill for some years, I understood why his published poetry had dried up earlier. By then I had his few poetry collections and was familiar with the poems and the places from which they arose. I felt I wanted to write of a man I had never met, and tease out further that thread that had drawn me to the place where he lived comfortably with his God, as priest, husband, father and simply man of prayer. A man who was attentive to all the joys that this life brings, as well as its sorrows and pain, with his acute sense of what energized and inspired others. Primarily I am entranced by his poetry, but a little of his prose also has a place in this book.

Any attempt to categorize the poems either by date or subject is likely to end unsatisfactorily, so I have settled for four broad chapters encompassing everything I would like to include. At the same time, and in all modesty, I pay tribute to the underlying faith of a priest of such gentle and sincere prayer and life. The four chapter titles are used in a broader sense than a strictly theological understanding, but that will be ascertained soon enough. I am no linguist nor literary critic, but I am a priest and an Anglican, which have imparted an insight into what makes the Church of England what it is and, perhaps more to the point regarding much of David's poetry, what it has been.

   I have been to many of the places in England, Ireland and the Holy Land in David's poetry, and have served in Winchester Diocese as did he. They are the few paths on which we intersect, and this book takes corresponding steps through the poems, and with them strings some thoughts together on faith, priesthood and life.

I

Annunciation

The Annunciation of the Blessed Virgin Mary

And the Angel came in unto her

from a painting by Sophie Hacker

Like an artist, she was always seeking
to make more room for light, and from herself
abandon all that blocked the strange bright thing.

It came as fire and moon and stars at night,
and touched by brightness she saw the dust ignite,
dancing in shafts of geometric light.

She read by it. It was the silent parable
on her skin. The texts were named in turn
as the shadow moved through the slow room.

Then came the day that Gabriel called her name
and to the light she swirled. Then wordless both,
the light enclosed her, and she all light became.

The wonder; for what before had never
been, never inched so close
to any human being, was done for ever.[3]

The Christian annunciation refers to the visit of the Angel Gabriel to the Blessed Virgin Mary to tell her that she is to be the mother of Jesus. In broader terms, we can see how every meeting that brings news, from one to another, is a kind of annunciation, and many are life enhancing, some are life changing. Christians have reflected long upon the importance of such encounters, from God walking with Adam in the Garden of Eden at the beginning of Genesis to the last strange and wonderful verses in the book of Revelation. As John writes, he expresses the vision of many nations and peoples, of all ages and races worshipping in the perpetual light of heaven.

Meetings with friends and memories of historical figures, imagined events and remembered occasions of past meetings are features of numerous poems, through which David Scott brings to life characters he has known and loved, or from whom he has learnt and grown as a person and as a Christian priest. I bring a few of these to bear on my encounter with David's poetry to illustrate a trait in priestly life, whence ministry is shared and, through the path of reminiscence, faith is shared and renewed. There is a gentle wisdom in many of these meetings. Some are even tangential and require a step or two of our own to complete the encounter, and so bring home the emotion and importance of what he notices and reflects in the poem.

David approaches St John of the Cross through the weather marking the edge of his clothing, the turn of his hand on a pen, the towers of Avila, reaching into the *Spiritual Canticle of the Soul*, which holds both the poetry of St John of the Cross related directly to the Song of Songs, and a detailed commentary on it. David's response to the beauty and depth of the text concludes, with carefully phrased allusion: 'I would glance to notice shifts of sun and shadow / of the alternating poetry and prose in you.'[4]

The poetry of contrast is symbolic of meetings, and illustrated by David in ways that bring a poignancy to situations that might otherwise appear as commonplace or even odd. Once more, in mind of Avila, Teresa is transferred from Spain to a November seaside with breakwaters, golf links, an early evening game of bridge, all within 'a bluish, evening mist'. That Carmelite spirituality can be so well expressed from simple objects and intentions sits lightly in this poem of bleached timber 'purified / by a century of salt pounding tide'. How brilliant is that? Falling sun and wounded heart, the golfer misjudging the camber of a green and the longing of Teresa's eyes, dried rosemary and darts that score and mark – with all the internal and double meanings that express more than prose could manage – are held in check in the poem 'A Walk with St Teresa of Avila'.[5]

Continuing the monastic theme, ostensibly with a lighter touch, 'A Nun on the Platform' succeeds in bringing sight and sound to bear on thoughtful imagining:

Seeing a nun on a platform
gives the day a jolt,
like an act of kindness,
or a pain that halts.[6]

As David's observant eye becomes imaginative so he assumes an effect of seeing the nun which, of course, speaks more of his mind than her being. This is a meeting with a distance, an invisible barrier of something sacred and consequently special. He develops a sense of setting-aside-ness that is evident elsewhere, such as when 'Pablo Casals Plays to the Wall'.[7] This poem has no interlocutor, but rather relies for its impact on an imaginative audience. So neither of these poems are referencing a meeting as such, but there are plenty that do.[8] These poems (and there may be others that we can bracket with them, for there is no precise ordering here) speak directly of a significant meeting, or suggest that there has been one or more, between two people who share something of themselves in a way too deep for words without the aid of poetic intuition.

David would draw us back to the source of all true engagement, that of prayer and our daily conversation with the God we meet at a level beyond any other. In his *Moments of Prayer*, one of his prose gifts to us, he reflects on his ministry as a priest, and thus imparts more general principles for the life of prayer. He also provides us with the counsel of past figures of importance to the Church and to him personally. Among these, Lancelot Andrewes is a towering figure. David is very much taken with his words and the power that words contain to inspire and engage further thought. In *Sacred Tongues* he reflects on Andrewes' sermons, and how he would:

> often dwell on the world contained within the letters of a single word. It was his way of meditating on the truth contained within them ... noting, as with a coin, how long it had been in use, and whose image, so to speak, was graven into it, what truth, and what reality lay within it.[9]

There is a sense of annunciation in all of this: the source of prayer, the source of reality behind a word or phrase, the combination of an active mind and an engaging thought. Or we might understand it as an inspired message, whether prophetic or sublime, that opens a door or window, however we might interpret it, to possibility, divine action or substantial life-affirming change. David gives an important example of this in the meeting of Mary Magdalene with Jesus on the first Easter morning. He constructs a piece of drama from a sermon preached on 16 April 1620 (Easter Day that year) by Lancelot Andrewes, which teases out and illuminates the account from the Fourth Gospel, which is so well known and the appointed reading for that Sunday. Those who are aware only of the poetry of David Scott may be pleasantly surprised by this piece of genius.

Andrewes appears in the dramatic text as commentator and narrator, and he demonstrates through him how it is that Mary Magdalene's life is resurrected in that dawn meeting, in direct consequence of the rising of Jesus from the dead:

Andrewes: 'What was her joy? He that was thought lost ...'
Magdalene: 'Is found again.'
Andrewes: 'And found not as he was sought for, not a dead body –'

Magdalene: 'But a living soul, nay, a quickened me and my spirits, that were as good as dead.'
Andrewes: 'You thought you should have come to Christ's resurrection today ...'
Magdalene: 'And so you do. But not to his alone, but even to my resurrection too. For in very deed, a kind of resurrection it is, is wrought in me; revived as it were and raised from a dead and drooping, to a lively and cheerful estate. The Gardener has done his part, made me all green on a sudden.'[10]

The gorgeous juxtaposition of Andrewes' voice with Mary's reflection, combined with Jesus as both Lord and 'Gardener', once again draws our eyes and sense of the spiritual reality on to ourselves, which is surely the point of Andrewes' brilliant sermon and illuminates a sense of annunciation that carries both revelation and message so dramatically and deeply.

Having gained a sense of powerful message delivered through context and word – in this case the life that is electrified with newness through the unique experience of witnessing the resurrection of Christ – it seems trite to glance at lesser meetings that express a sense of annunciation too. However, as they also tangentially demonstrate emotion and revelation on a human level, I shall run through some of David's meetings and remembrances.

In 'For John Ball' the vehicle of revelation is captured in the words 'you sat still; and had a private voice / which only carried as far as it needed'. It seems that there is a double meaning included in this expression of familiarity and friendship. Priests may have a naturally cohesive language of their own, and John Ball was a priest with an affinity for David Scott. And that affinity was not only mutual, it was understood in the message that was delivered in a very particular way, revealed in the words 'still', 'private' and the phrase 'as far as it needed'. Mary, the mother of the Lord, may have heard Gabriel, as 'touched by brightness she saw the dust ignite, / dancing in shafts of geometric light'. And Mary Magdalene was made 'all green on a sudden', but this lesser meeting with John Ball communicates truth only so far as was necessary for that moment.

David Scott presents meetings that carry the import of a message in a way that allows the channel to play on our senses in an extraordinarily emotive way. 'For Martin' takes us to the wild and beautiful west of Ireland. This is a land of wide landscapes and dramatic features, from cliffs and mountains to strands and moorland. Yet what is chosen to translate the feeling of oneness and the proximity of mortal demise? It is the thorn and the flower of a gorse bush. These simple things are features familiar to all who recognize the pain and beauty that encompasses human life. The reader is left not knowing what Martin did or said that meant so much to the grateful author of this poem, but it is enough to understand the engagement that channels the emotions experienced through the simple observations of 'torn cloth and trammelled thread'.

'For Brother Jonathan' we are given the fact, in an amplification of the title, that he died, having been washed out to sea. This motif of water is the feature of the poem's verses that holds the sense of what, in life and death, Brother Jonathan was to those who knew him. It appears at the beginning, with surely a baptismal reference, of allowing the sea to be experienced right over him. But then, mysteriously, Jonathan drew David from the imagination of quiet and the sea being all needful, to the harsher realities of polishing floors, narrow staircases and backache. Here are echoes of George Herbert and the composite nature of spiritual life committed to the God of love. The damp servers' albs, wet tents, sweaty under a heavy habit, are all there on the way to the shore of an empty beach. This poem reveals something similar to 'For Martin', if less mysteriously, but still, the poetry of loss becomes the conduit of more than just an emotional response. The lessons, albeit gradual and gaining traction with age and experience, have brought the transient to illuminate and help to understand what Christians understand of the eternal.

ANNUNCIATION

Exploring the facets of 'annunciation' refers us back to that of Gabriel to Mary, of light and vision and promise and hope, and underlying everything is the acceptance of the reality of miracle. Hidden within this is the 'why me' of humility, so justly surrounding the person of Mary, especially at the moment of receiving the news, and further reflected in the words of the Magnificat. With other meetings, both real and imagined, in David Scott's poems, a picture can be constructed that draws threads of what miracles dialogue can declare when lived in faith, love and hope.

'For Norman Nicholson' is a poem that demonstrates that annunciation found within dialogue conveys considerably more than a single message, as context and basic humanity are so revealing. This poem for the much-loved, Millom-born poet has interwoven conversations, including the glory of the natural world held within the 'silent doom / of Windscale'. But there is something of the issues of today being met with life of a century ago, and through the lens of a film set. Just a word or two draws our attention to the reality of what is lost, or potentially lost: ordinary village streets with shops and a chapel, with 'So many corners to lean against'. The message enunciated, if not annunciated, is of the fragile remains of past life showing forth the vulnerable aspects of humanity, and the consequences of human carelessness or folly in shedding what is unwanted or risking what is of ageless beauty and worth. And for what? So the question is raised without the answer. The responsibility of finding the answer is handed to the reader or hearer of the poem, in memory of an honoured figure whose own concern is part of the ongoing dialogue.

While we traverse this countryside of the memorial poems of David Scott, my attention is grabbed with rereading 'For Pete Laver'. This is set in Grasmere, a place beloved of poets and all who love the Lake District and its poets, especially William Wordsworth. The scene is set in sunshine and showers as David recalls both happy memories and unaccountable tears. There is laughter and seriousness too, as the recollection of a car reversed into the River Derwent is paralleled with tracing the words on a tombstone. The internal rhythm of the poem is typical of the touching, breath-of-God-as-wind-across-the-grasses-of-a-meadow, which catches one unawares and leaves one with a smile and a slightly raised heart-rate. What is lost is found. But then, in 'For Frances Horovitz', the finding is in collecting images. The tracing is not with finger on stone, but with the eye gathering them like 'a necklace'. This is a poem with a hidden subtext, of which the uninformed reader can but guess. The wall with its crevices is probably Hadrian's Wall, which formed the northern boundary of the Roman Empire, but crevices also suggest the Western Wall in Jerusalem, which is also a transitional barrier as well as a place of pilgrimage and remembrance. The 'tight sweater' suggests compression and struggle, as well as revelation and release in a poem with suitably tightly written observation through layers of interpretation hung on deep personal remembrance to an oblique but most interesting end.

'With Miggy at Skelwith Force' brings us into an emotional country of a particularly personal recollection to Scott. Here is a place of safe memory, of happiness, linked both to the child and the grown David, resting in security spelt in placid water before the fall, then in the refreshing and renewing 'bridal veil of spume'. What touches the reader is what touches in a different way the author. It is the 'single harebell'. Power and fragility together, and that composition is, in itself, able to move hearts and minds tuned to the flow of life, in all its capacity to surprise, shock and entwine with joy and love. This is a lovely poem.

The need to communicate is implied in annunciation, and its absence is one of the paradoxes of the reference in the Bible to those who will hear but not hear, will see but not see, will understand but not understand. The texts that demonstrate that God does not always communicate, because of the state of heart and mind of the person or family or nation, are in their own way as important as those that state clearly the message that is being imparted to the chosen servant who is faithful, open and attentive to the word of God. How we fail to communicate with one another when there appear to be blockages between people is frequently referred to as not being on the same wavelength. It calls upon a need to adjust the ability to hear from both sides. The poem 'On Not Knowing R. S. Thomas' demonstrates an attempt by both poets to communicate, and, as in the subject matter of many R. S. Thomas poems, there is a sense that understanding is communicating by the absence of certainty, the darkness rather than the light, the tangential implication rather than wordy precision. The poem describes an understandable awkwardness between them. Yet what is there holds our attention perfectly, for as with our attempt to engage so they met in familiar places, and not fleetingly. It was over three days. David the more casual, but 'both hiding, both awkward'. So the 'Not Knowing' with capital letters beginning each word holds the essence of R. S. Thomas as poet and person. Reflecting R. S. Thomas' chosen retirement home near the sea at Y Rhiw on the Llŷn Peninsula, David Scott chooses to reference the wind, the 'sea's drone' and the glory that is in the hiddenness – surely another double meaning.

Somewhere tucked among my notebooks I have a reminder of the lectures that John Fenton gave to the clergy of Winchester Diocese on St John's Gospel. These remain in my memory as one of the most notable events of all the in-service sessions organized for the priests of any diocese in which I have served. In the poem 'Canon Fenton, Theologian', David Scott refers to this biblical scholar's fascination with the ending of St Mark's Gospel. He also uses the words 'narrows down', which appear in a much earlier, and one of my favourites of all David's poems, 'Reading Party',[11] in which priests on retreat 'narrow down the glory' that is all around them in the landscape of the Lake District by being fixated on their own ecclesiastical finery. In 'Canon Fenton, Theologian', David is reflecting on Fenton's view that faith itself can narrow down the power 'of most things, this side of the future'. If David is considering existentially, and apparently is in tune with the implication, the 'see-sawing / of one foot to another' through our mortal existence, of which faith is the spiritual element, does dull the senses to what is to come as light perpetual shines 'that brooks no eulogy'. As suits the person who is the subject of this poem, this piece is a deeply theological one, which renders the attempt at eulogy finely indeed.

'Miss Taylor, Church Organist' presents an altogether lighter atmosphere; of one whose eccentricities may have caused amusement, but whose toughness could produce at the right moment such a look able to shrivel up the most self-confident with a steely glance. It brings us to an aspect of annunciation that is not easy to accept, though its presence is more experienced than admitted: the perception of failure in the face of another's gifts or success of what may be seen as good fortune. Some people just seem to be lucky; others are grafters and paddle their own canoe and succeed by sheer power of determination, and can become the butt of jokes and carry on regardless. There is discomfort for the sensitive in all of this, and even in contemplating it with affection. All of which hovers around the underlying fear of an insecure sense of worth and general vulnerability. The emotions that press in on the sensitive soul include pity and heartache, with the anxious feeling that that is not the reaction to another person that demonstrates respect and high regard, but rather a kind of embarrassed superiority of which the observer is deeply ashamed and wants to disown. But then there is the fear of failure.

David Scott teases out this thought in one of his books. Not unexpectedly it is in *The Mind of Christ*. Before he gets to that particular subject he explores another lesson, that of finding stillness and silence as a young man, and thereby gives me the title of this book. David takes us back to the last years of his school days and to a very simple event that left a deep impression. He and another pupil accompanied the school chaplain to pick up the preacher for Sunday evensong. It was a journey into the wilds and eventually to a converted stable block of what had been a great house, now a ruin except for this converted outbuilding, that had been built as a monastic settlement. But the point that he makes is that the founder, an Anglican monk called William Sirr (aka William of Glasshampton), had lived there on his own most of the time from 1918 to 1936, with a few joining him from time to time but no one staying. The monastic centre at Glasshampton was taken over by the Franciscans, from where the preacher was to be collected on the afternoon in 1965. The reason why David Scott tells the story relates to the last day of William Sirr's tenancy of the place, which we shall come to in a moment. But first was the relating of the arrival at the place and the affect it had on him. David speaks of the moment when the Land Rover engine was switched off by the chaplain who was driving:

> He stopped just so we could hear the stillness. It was a sort of deep stillness I had never heard before. Life up till then had never consciously just stopped. School was busy and noisy and silence was always a command or a punishment. This was freedom and love. This was a bath of silence which began from nothingness and then moved into distant birdsong; and even that didn't break the silence – it was part of it.[12]

There is no doubt in my mind that this was a formative moment for David, and he couples it with a reference to the last day of William Sirr at this place. He was being collected and taken to where he could be cared for, as he had fallen ill. The Revd Sidney King was called upon to make the pick-up. The piece that is quoted in *The Mind of Christ* at this point is from Geoffrey Curtis' book of 1947, *William of Glasshampton*. It is worth quoting in full, as it is by David, because it too left an impression on him, who knew the place from the schooldays visit in 1965:

> As the years went on and I saw the Monastery take its form – the cells for Monks all prepared and yet no Monks – I ceased to enquire if any fresh Postulants had come, feeling it must be painful for him to speak of it. On this last morning

when I saw him on his bed his face lit up in welcome. I asked him if I might pray with him, I knelt at what was his last prayer in the Monastery. I commended him to God and besought God's peace upon him.

When I rose from my knees he said, looking me straight in the face, serene and untroubled, apropos of nothing said in the interview or in the prayers, *'We must not mind being a failure – Our Lord died on the Cross a failure.'* Words I can never forget, nor the tone of his serene, quiet repose in the Will of God. I knew in the absolute surrender of his will to God, he had entered into the victorious mind of our Saviour on the Cross and knew the ineffable peace which only the saints very near to God can know; and into which nothing can break or destroy.[13]

In this particular case, the significant meeting that David Scott alludes to is not one of which he is a party, but through that of two other people, both at heart like-spirits, the inner resonance of feeling is transmitted and an important message received and understood. Even as I encapsulate the themes of some of the poetry and prose works of David Scott within a universal theme, I want to disentangle them and start again. And yet some strong threads are teased out by so doing, and so I shall proceed to the last poem under this section, 'Together: An Elegy'. With this poem I shall move on from comment on the specific genre of David's work that involves the illustrative meetings of individuals, and that announces something within their dialogue. They pop up within other of Scott's works, of course, without being specific to them. But within the still centre of these poems – which resonate most deeply with the soul in tune with the Magnificat and its themes of revelation, commitment, wonder and hope – there rests a common sense of the exposé of the love and justice that resides in the heart of God. There is enough in these poems to stir the will to further exploration and endeavour and to place them where they should be, in the conscious devotional legacy of the universal Church.

ANNUNCIATION

What do I make of 'Together: An Elegy'? Someone could, no doubt, indicate why this intimate poem was penned in the way it was. What event prompted it is, in a way, not the point at issue. Judge Derek Stanley died after a short illness at the age of 59. He was known to uphold the highest of standards in both his professional and personal life. The poem responds to this not as an observation but in response to the reaction that David Scott felt in his presence and within the matter of their meeting. As the poem unfolds so does the emotion of 'Why not me?' of someone of my own age and in the midst of his working life dying, while I, of lesser worth in my own eyes, continue to live. The conclusion is hopeful and loving. There is no parting that is beyond the grace of God; no true love that can be broken; no lesson that need be lost. What Derek Stanley and David Scott meant to one another holds its meaning eternally.

In so far as meetings reveal things to those who come together, so detecting something of those revelations, through the vehicle of the poetry of one party in the meeting, has an extraordinary power to trigger emotions, memories, hopes and challenges within the heart and mind of the reader. It is truly a kind of annunciation, with layer upon layer of resonance, as music can be experienced at different levels and in different moods. I am interested especially in what I am hearing of David Scott's faith. He has been likened to other poet-priests, particularly George Herbert. I haven't always found that analogy as meaningful as perhaps I do now, having got lost somewhere in comparing the style of the poetry itself. However, further on and reading more deeply into the poems I am finding that the ongoing dialogues between sacred and secular, physical and spiritual, day and night, light and darkness, stillness and activity, noise and silence – all of these things that we are inclined to polarize – are never entirely separated and treated as mutually opposed in Scott's mind. The truth is always somewhere in the meeting and the transference of meaning held in the tension. If it is also true that nothing is perfectly reconciled in this life except in the person of Jesus

Christ, then we too must work within the costly grace that is the work of reconciliation, where a degree of tension is what maintains the constant search for perfect love, an unresting striving for justice in a world of injustice, and ultimately for that peace that passes our understanding. It is here that I see the parallel with George Herbert, as identifying the place one needs to occupy, and the state of mind, in prayer and daily life, that requires faith, hope and love, with the emphasis, as with St Paul, on the pre-eminence of the latter.

We are not, of course, the first to discover these things, and revelation and annunciation come in different ways, something that Elizabeth's husband Zechariah discovered at much the same time that Joseph was challenged with Mary's mysterious news. The angel has such a crucial role, and language is a vehicle of interpretation, as in the poem 'The Awe that Falls on Language',[14] 'like Zechariah waiting for his new born son / for whom he had no words. / God took his time to present the child, / and for the bell and tongue to be unstrung.'

The ordinary screens not the things of eternity, but rather can be exquisitely revealing. Let us end this chapter and begin the next with the poet and artist David Jones, with whom David Scott has an obvious affinity, with two extraordinarily poignant poems:

A David Jones Annunciation

In such an ordinary room
the angel came skidding to rest:
she on a bench of prayer
he to get news off his chest.

Arrivals can happen like that
on the day you least expect,
when the washing's on the line
and you've no idea what's next.

ANNUNCIATION

He was such a gentle angel
with a lily in his hand,
and his eyes so meekly angled
you have to understand.

The King is in search of a kingdom;
the time to be born is soon,
and God wants you to house him
in the byre of your womb.

She sat as still as the chair
staring at the cool, tiled floor
and the silence was deeper there,
than she'd ever heard before.

Neither knew how to break it.
Neither was wanting to press.
It was probably only a minute
but it felt like an hour to say 'yes'.

'Yes' was the shape of the farmhouse.
'Yes' were the trunks of the trees.
'Yes' was the gate on its hinges.
'Yes' brought the world to its knees.[15]

2

Nativity

A David Jones Nativity
(*Gentilis animetur*)

All four hooves, Welsh as a pony on hill
are inches off the frosted ground. They skip
for a fish tight saviour who is swathed in stillness
between apple breast and pillow of hair.
Come to look at it, all are off the ground:
cow and ladle, shepherdess and lute,
bits of floating Latin, but all stock still,
as if playing statues.

I am waiting for the cockerel to spill
its redness on the page to Botticelli up the colour
and set the world in motion, from out of winter
into summer. Then the snow will melt
and who knows what the sun might loose them into.[16]

David Jones is perhaps best known today for his long wartime poem *In Parenthesis*. However, his drawings are a discovery waiting to be made for many of us. The imagination that lies behind all of the nativity artwork of Jones is stimulating and exciting. The drawing that David Scott reflects on in his poem is the busiest of them all, but also, as with Craigie Aitchison's crucifixion art, it and all of the nativity pictures are full of character and unusual perspective. As with the poem, the drawing is not for the casual glance. There is enough in it for hours and hours of perusal; each line and area of shading, angle of sight and facial expression, unexpected object and hint of something not quite there, but suggested, should keep us happily occupied for some time. And happy is an important description of this drawing, for it is no stylized composition for the appreciation of the devout, but a joyous and exuberant expression of the coming of the Saviour. It is an earthy incarnation and claims its reality.

In the poem based on this nativity, as with that on the annunciation, David Scott places movement, or the lack of it, centrally. There is stillness in both, and a lightness of placement of the characters that suggests the Spirit of God blowing through the scenes. David emphasizes the skip, the pillow, the tightness of the swathing, but the contrasting floating of the Latin; everything off the ground yet everything still as statues. The whole scene awaits something more; it is pregnant with life and motion and the music of the lute, as snow is melted in the sun and those playing statues are loosed into activity.

This poem starts us into a series of poems that loosely can be gathered around the theme of releasing into new life, opportunity and action. I shall start with 'Churchyard under Snow',[17] which is characteristically full of Scott's illusion to what has been and what will remain. This is an underlying thread in many poems. The simple action, such as shaking snow off a wreath, is enough to bring to mind warm days and a summer dress, recalling a life in the midst of a churchyard of graves, holding an individual, yes, as they have been, but also implying that their life is as our love holds them, not as the frozen earth encases their mortal remains. He emphasizes this with the use of 'cold' and 'cutting wind', but also the reality of mortality in the 'unimaginable weathering'. All in all it is an introduction to a powerful impression of life, eternity, joy and love.

If 'Churchyard under Snow' gives birth to an idea, there are numerous Scott poems that create a sense of discovery linked to a moment, an event or an unfolding of life. One of my favourite of all the poems is 'Reading Party'.[18] I have quoted this several times while leading retreats, especially with a group that I know are reluctant to leave their parishes or suspend their routine. The location is a house 'by Windermere' that is large enough to hold the party of priests and have its own library too. Enough one would imagine for walking and convivial sharing of the beauty of the place, some ecclesiastical chat, no doubt, but more readily their eyes must have been raised to the hills and their walks filled with the susurration of the lake water on the shore. But no, it took a week for them to notice and appreciate that the nature-scape was informing their theology, and 'longer still to skim a pebble on the lake'.

Discovery lies across two pages of *A Quiet Gathering*, with the poems 'David Livingstone on the Eve of Discovering the Victoria Falls' and 'The Presbytery Cellar'.[19] In both poems David Scott uses words to create a sense of darkness from which very simple symbols of something much greater, of awe and mystery, appear. With 'David Livingstone' we read of him poring over his 'Greek text of Luke' by the light of a lamp, laboriously lit with a 'flint-lock'. But the wonder of the great falls are lying in the words seen, imagined, heard and repeated: thunder, smoke, waiting, rainbow, noise, roar, smoke (again), thunderous, 'more like fire than water', for the discovery is about to burst upon him, as he finds on the next day, 'what water burns, what fire ignites both rainbows'. In the cellar of the old presbytery there is the clutter of 'brown junk', as Scott need not describe the tarnished brass, the dark and dusty woodwork, the dodgy electrics, the statues and the suitcases that have not seen the light of day for a very long time, the rest 'yellowing', the books, not just books but 'copies of the Fathers / sent from the Mother House'. That is a nice little touch that encapsulates it all. But there are two things for which the priests come every year: the crib for Christmas and patches and glue to mend a tyre. The discovery of the birth of the Saviour is indeed among the mundane and the need to repair what is broken.

The sad poem 'Village Organist' also ends at Christmas. From girl to aged and infirm woman, the village organist's life is laid out in a series of verses that build towards what we know must happen, as she faces one challenge after another, until she becomes less and less able to manage the organ at all, 'as one finger / after another went permanently cream', and her final service came between her and her sleep; ever expected to be a climax, it was to be a children's Christmas event, but it never happened, all was left 'with the note book, her glasses, and her pencil'.[20]

Although not strictly any form of nativity, a number of David Scott's poems push the boundaries of discovery to the touching edge of some sense of birthing of an idea, a concept; perhaps better, a feeling that something undeniably amazing is taking place, and all in the ordinary way of life that is simply influenced by something special, or beyond it. A good example of this is 'Botanical Gardens'.[21] This is a poem recalling a particular day, towards the end of which the author was slowly ushered out of a botanical garden. The neat order of the garden is contrasted with the disorder beyond its gates, which are about to be closed behind him. How this mystery works, he is not sure. There are Latin names, a shining hoe, evidence of work completed for the day. But there remains something it is impossible to explain, which has its source out of sight: 'It snaked back, like the pipes / in the Glass House, to a hidden tap.' Although David's feeling and understanding may seem incompatible with, or perhaps better, disconnected from, the experience of the visiting shepherds and wise men to the birthplace of Jesus, there was a disturbance in this human-created Eden, which brought a conscious parallel to something newborn. There is within it the contemplation, carefully woven into the poem, of order within disorder, and of what is open to sight being a mysterious and awesome expression of something infinitely more vital and important than what was before his eyes. A child in swaddling clothes and lying in a manger may hold incarnate life, not just subjectively projected by the observer, as somehow David's inner perception or sixth sense, a spiritual enlightenment that was not self-wrought. I may not have his layers of meaning quite right, but the secret of the place (at whatever level he under-

NATIVITY

stood what was hidden) remains where he felt it, and knew it. Some mystery was new-found for him, snaking back to an undisclosed source.

There is frequently something more in David's poems that is bringing a truth to light in the midst of the entirely mundane, the routine, just carrying on for ever, for that is how it is – or was. Take the 8.00 a.m. Sunday tradition in many churches, not that many years prior to the Covid-19 pandemic. A small and faithful congregation would join the priest for a Book of Common Prayer Service of Holy Communion. There would be no sermon, no variables, no change. It is all there, in 'Early Communion'.[22] It must have been close to Christmas, perhaps very early in the New Year, as the snow was brushed from the 'leaning board', declaring the time and nature of the service, with the 'only variables' being the change in his pocket for the collection and 'the winter jasmine above the holy table'. Once again the revelation of the mystery of God transforming the everyday to a vehicle of spiritual light is evident.

More obviously, as it is directly referencing the sacramental, 'A Long Way from Bread' catalogues the ways of making bread and its use in becoming holy, so getting the bread right is of the utmost concern. A similarly direct poem is 'Eyes'.[23] There is most certainly a sense of the eye-opening such as we witness in all of the poems in this chapter, as incarnation, discovery, recognition and the recalibration of the mundane reveal themselves. But 'Eyes' approaches the experience of seeing itself, as among the greatest of wonders and what they show us of another, whether a stranger in the crowd or a loved brother or sister: 'God of the one strand of hair, are you also / God of the one look, of the glance, of the glimpse?'

Compared with direct allusions to the cross, David Scott's poetry related specifically to Christ's birth is thin, but the Italianate touch of 'A Botticelli Nativity' does take us to the luxuriance of the Kings if not to the poverty of the stable. The mounts are horses, the crumbling walls are seeded with Florentine flowers. The beauty extolled in the late fifteenth and early sixteenth centuries of Renaissance Europe is unveiled in paint and poetry. This is, as Scott records, 'Medici Bethlehem', and there is colour everywhere comparing in the mind, which still holds David Jones' nativity clearly, the glory of human kingship with the breath of the divine. Mary is a 'shy / Madonna, and the peacock preens the sky'.[24]

The ground is surer that beats the lifeless into the shadows while revealing the strength of the new and zestful. Though this general principle will always be seen in a nativity, by its very nature the general theme appears elsewhere too, such as in 'Abbey Ruins'[25] and even 'Castlerigg Songs'.[26] The first hints at a birth with its girls dancing and the 'ruin, like a shell cracked open, lay / aghast at their experiment with air', while the second contrasts the stones, of 'no illumination; / no face, no feature', with the solidity of the stone itself, and the elemental things of earth and air, but concludes simply with 'being born, death'.

Before looking at further examples of poems insinuating into situations quite normal and mundane the injection of life that is either obviously of eternity or hints strongly that the author imagines it to be or tend that way, consciously or otherwise, let us consider the theological insight that is being revealed. Faith demands that God revealed to us in Jesus Christ is reconciling the world of mortality, sin and human failure to the divine life, stimulated by and existing in and through love and justice. Mercy, compassion, grace, peace and hope are all of the experience of the Christian whose love is called out to bear upon God who loved us first and from the beginning of creation, and upon our neighbour as being the object of our energy, released through forgiveness, restitution and renewal. The significant events of Christ's earthly life are illustrative of this outcome, and those closest to him are inspired by his Spirit and know failure as well as joy, for humanity is both vulnerable and glorious, of such matter we are made.

Within the poems gathered around a general heading (my title, I hasten to add) of prayer and ministry, the discovery of the essence of Christian outlook and action in the day to day, including a bent towards wisdom and truth, as far as such are understood as being held by the divine whether from the literature of the Scriptures or from the commonly accepted outcome of dwelling upon them while reflecting on life, there is the quiet certainty of faith, tested and lived. However, in a more directly analytical description of what is happening to us as we acknowledge and embrace our humanity, in *The Mind of Christ*, Scott talks of the nature of humanity as requiring separation from God.[27]

> In the mind of God, can we say, this was an essential separation in order to bring the world back to himself. Jesus was God's Son and the responsibility of the Son was to bring the world back into relationship with the Father.[28]

The poem in question for David Scott is not one of his own, but what he reads of St Paul in Philippians 2.7–8:

> being born in human likeness ...
> And being found in human form,
> he humbled himself
> and became obedient to the point of death –
> even death on a cross.[29]

The comment on these verses relates to the incarnation bringing us down with Christ, 'physically sharing in the descent',[30] yet – and this is the interesting reflection – David Scott, in touching on the cross at this point, sees in it a drawing of humanity heavenward, as the cross has both vertical and horizontal aspects. 'The cross lifts our eyes and our hearts upward as it lifted Jesus and we prepare with him for the ascent to the Father.'[31] After quoting further verses from Philippians 2 relating to God raising Jesus and humanity bending the knee at his name, Scott adds an important paragraph that I include here in its entirety:

> It seems awkward treating Christ as a paradigm for everything we do in this life, as if every little thing has so much importance. Perhaps we don't have to personalize all

this too quickly, but spend time thanking God that Christ was able to do it for us. Generally we live on a more simple domestic level making small acts of humility, which are often all too easy to achieve. It is far more useful to reflect on those who live lives of suffering love, even when everything is stacked against them. We think of mothers who have to watch their children die of AIDS or starvation, for want of water or medical resources. The notion of humbling is not glamorous. To follow Christ is to be, in any situation, open to a service that drains from us spiritual strength and empties us of it because we let it flow out to another. We do this not because we know in our mind that it is the way of Christ and therefore might reap its benefits, but because of the love of Christ which means we can do no other. The effect of our actions, and the future, are in God's hands.[32]

Towards the end of Scott's *Selected Poems* we find a number of poems that can be placed under the general heading of prayer and ministry, to which his reflections on the fact of Christ embracing humanity are paramount, with the outcome described in the paragraph as quoted. Taking them one by one, the first doesn't quite fit by title but it does in essence, namely 'A Quaker Sitting'.[33] This poem holds the frequent David Scott theme of 'Silence' centrally, unsurprisingly. What is less expected is the tension that he observes existing in the figure before, of a man at prayer. While beginning with the thought that the Quaker is sitting 'relaxed on a hard chair', he imagines that he is needing to 'uncoil within'; he may speak from 'a store of words he has / gathered over the years', while the observation is around the contact of hard surfaces in the room, and between the hands and face of the man at prayer, bringing to mind 'the conscientious objector / and the Ambulance Corps, frugality, / evening classes at The Settlement / and household pain'. Here we have humanity at Christ's call, faithfully looking to what is right, but too tense to love. The closing words of the poem surprise us really: 'I would title it "Wisdom Heaped".'

Moving on to 'A Priest with the Bible',[34] we are with David as he observes himself rather than another. The poet is in that tantalizing, playful mood that puts a smile on the reader's face, whatever the subject matter. He is on the poetry of the Old Testament and its relationship to Wisdom; that is, Wisdom as Christ, incarnate Son and human relation, foreseen centuries before; less Wisdom Heaped, more like Wisdom's Shape. Scott trips lightly across Ruth and Samuel, through the Song of Songs, 'with its ramparts and gazelles, / cinnamon, frankincense, / and its sheer hard won delight / between he and she', but then across the page he actually bids us not to skip lightly through the generations of Christ's human ancestors, for he wants us to notice the meetings and the beauty too; the reality of 'surprise births', and how and why David wept for Absalom, and Mary stood at the cross of her son. Scott reminds us in his own way of his own words elsewhere: 'The notion of humbling is not glamorous.'[35]

'A Priest in a New Parish'[36] is also a reflection from the beginning of the Scotts' move to Winchester. Those who know of the beauty and purity of the Hampshire chalk stream and the presence of clear running water all around the City of Winchester (though brought somewhat down to earth in Roger Deakin's *Waterlog*) will have no difficulty in understanding the fascination with these waterways as the priest in his new parish is gently lulled by the quiet flowing and the rushing channels, as Scott feels it, 'running / like fingers through my hair'. Here is a kind of new birth, such as priests discover in the move to new people, new home, new place of work, life and experience. 'They choose us', he reflects when considering why they made the move, but the poem centres on the movement of the water, and brings the nearness of it to all he does and is in both its life-giving and cleansing capacities. This is built into the history of the place too. As Christ's birth didn't just happen in a random way in a disconnected place to an insignificant human family, so prayer and ministry in the name of Jesus Christ is not random either. It is what 'leaps out / unexpectedly' as water appears and disappears, here exposed and busy with ducks and swans, there hidden in culverts and private demesnes. The river, Scott says, helps him to find his voice as he listens to 'this water's / mute capacity to sing'.

The capacity to surprise is also to be discovered in the next poem in the *Selected Poems*, again within my bracket of prayer and ministry. It is a poem called 'A Priest at the Crematorium',[37] and relates an occasion when the author was conducting the funeral of a man whose life work was delivering groceries, and whose mourners were 'in awkward suits', and 'nipping their fags'. Many of us know exactly the scene that lay before the priest that day, and the reassuring prayers and liturgical movement that allowed the family their moments of grief in such a place of regulated time and formalized service. It was then with surprise that towards the second chapel on the crematorium site there seemed in contrast to be a simple and colourful procession flowing 'like candles on a river'. The sight that caught his eye seemed out of place. Twenty sari-clothed women, 'so graceful', while seeing 'their veils catching / and releasing the sun'. Once more, and most obviously here, the proclamation of life in the midst of death, taking place in a chapel where words declare that very thing, also meets the surprise of the unexpected event allegorically announcing the same thing.

'A Priest at the Door'[38] brings the reality of perceived usefulness or otherwise of the priest to those who enter the church building to the fore. What is the purpose or need that is fulfilled by the presence of a priest? There are no animals to sacrifice as in Old Testament times, no daily rituals with incense and slaughter and much blood to fling towards the altar, ceremonial clothes to wear and curtains to close on a priest knowing clearly his role. Now, male or female, no matter which, will 'get books and papers / snippets of news, and the magazine'. David Scott is touching on the intangible nature of contemporary priestly life, without that ritual of sacrifice so familiar in pre-Christian times, or even the defined schedule of the monastic rule, and in reflecting that an Anglican priest has little that is identifiable in their role he says, 'I have only the agony / of knowing I have little, / and the slow job of resisting / any attempt to make it more.'

The back cover blurb of Scott's *Selected Poems* includes the following words:

> David Scott's poetry evokes the delicate, intense qualities of rural England – its people and places, its wildlife, history and traditions. The pastoral nature of his daily work emerges in the later poems as a relish for detail, not trumpeted, but noticed for what it is worth.

The comment is very clearly borne out not only in 'A Priest at the Door' but in others too, including 'A Priest in a Bookshop',[39] which betrays a particularly arcane drift of mind and heart while the main focus of the reason for him being there is temporally lost, to the point of wondering why he is there at all. Or is it? Can it be that this questioning whether high up a bookshop ladder or scrambling around the floor, searching, is expressing not so much a particular need but a more general one, one that forms around other features of no importance in the shop, 'fungus in the cracks, / and the delicate skulls of birds'? This 'pastoral nature' in its widest and most reflective sense is taken further in a more specific mode of description by the following poem in the collection, 'A Priest at Prayer'.[40] This is an important poem for the understanding of how that 'pastoral nature' comes to express itself in the intimacy of prayer. It is a revealing statement that says more than the words declare. I shall analyse it line by line, for this poem helps illuminate David Scott's insistence that 'To follow Christ is to be, in any situation, open to a service that drains from us spiritual strength and empties us of it because we let it flow out to another', quoted above from *The Mind of Christ*.

The opening of 'A Priest at Prayer' runs as follows: 'From prayer to prayer involves / a dwindling, a way of being / that accounts for weariness.' David acknowledges that as a priest he is coming to the point of prayer through an experience of 'dwindling', subconsciously if not with complete awareness, and that this 'accounts for weariness'. It indicates both the state of his mind and heart, and perhaps experienced physically too, but less that, I think, than in the spiritual weariness in offering prayer; an emptying that seeks restoration and renewal. The reason is in having given of himself in pastoral work he is applying that giving to prayer too, but, 'and this is vitally important', the prayer is restorative. How does David Scott describe the way this happens? By these words: 'a regular / drawing in and letting out of breath; / the planting of a word and its forgetting, / a close examination of what is there / until it isn't, a candle flame beating air, / love meeting Love'.

I believe that David must have agonized over the words of this poem for some time, wondering how he was going to explain to a reader or hearer what lay in his heart as he turned to pray; how it affected him, and how he saw its operation and inner transforming. He is giving us three pictures describing the efficacy of prayer. The first is 'the planting of a word and its forgetting'. Is he forgetting the planting, or forgetting the word, or both? This is an interesting concept. My guess is that it is both, no matter whether this is a prayer of intercession or a prayer of confession. The 'forgetting' comes about because of the release that is experienced in leaving the issue in God or, as I should imagine it in David's heart and mind, *in Christ*. Holding that thought for a moment, we come to his second description, 'a close examination of what is there / until it isn't'. This is more specifically describing the disappearance of the issue, be it a prayer for something relating to himself or for another. It is best thought of as in the pain of childbirth, all-consuming until it has gone, because there is a birth, a transformation, a new life. This is a very powerful concept of how prayer works for a Christian whose whole demeanour in prayer is Christ-orientated. In other words, it is personal, bound up with a relationship so intimate that it is life-changing, red-hot or like a 'candle flame beating air'. These three metaphors are concluded and summed up with the words 'love meeting Love'. It is perfect. But let's see the end:

love meeting Love before the house wakes up;
space body-shaped, time vacated,
the passive tense, a waiting to receive,
out-of-bounds of what is right
or wrong, subject to being surprised
by God on briefest sight.

On an initial read this may seem less intense, and in a way that is true. The release of the forgetting and the conclusion that what has been agonized over is now in the compassionate and merciful arms of the Almighty leaves the 'love meeting Love' forming not only the mid-point of the poem but the moment in which the dwindling and the weariness experience some restitution. The house waking up is not simply an addition to complete the line or to let us know that David prayed early before the family got up each day: it is hinting at the daily course of life as receiving, as an infant is handed and positioned, unaware, by a midwife to a mother after she has given birth; entirely the baby is receiving, entirely the baby knows no right or wrong, entirely the moment is timeless, passive and the end of a painful wait, but the miracle of birth, ever a surprise, brings a moment of intense joy.

'A Priest at Prayer' is just 13 short lines. It encapsulates the essence of prayer in its most reflective mood and understanding. It is a lesson in theological expression that needs time to be disentangled and dwelt upon, but it is consequently subtle and nuanced and not readily taught. Rather, as with all works on prayer, they have a life of their own. More importantly, they are or should be treated as a stepping stone to the real thing, which can only be discovered by each individual alone. The poem may reflect a kind of birth, but its genius is that it points the way to another.

The harebell appears in at least three of David's poems, but most descriptively in 'In its substance is but air ...',[41] which is the title of the poem rather than a line within it. Its delicacy and inconsequence is of its nature; it has a thin stem, and often its head is blowing in the breeze on a wall or dusty turf, but it is a startling blue and a distinctly bell-shaped flower. He has an eye for this high-summer bloom, and to him its appearance is a sign of hope amid the chaos that is so much of this world. 'This delight, this silent sense of being / is a wonder', and the reason why I place this particular poem among those announcing birth of one kind or another. The harebell calls him; it is 'affirming'.

That light reflection on the tender and the beautiful I set between 'A Priest at Prayer' and 'Retirement'.[42] This latter piece surely is the poem that marks a transition for David, an acceptance that he had reached or knew he was reaching a point at which the familiar and the repetition of what had been was vital to his spiritual equilibrium. His struggle is evident; he fears to write anything, not knowing whether or not it is as he imagines; he converses with his soul. The sadness for the reader is in that unequal battle to seek poise, revive what his life is, be attentive, be calm and 'hope again to learn a love for others, / and of others love for me'. It is a poem of deep significance, and ultimately of faith in the underlying sense that all 'is settled back on God the pivot, / I the balance'. I am glad that this poem appears, placed apparently randomly, as it is, among the journeying home from a funeral, a reflection on a lifetime's talking on Christ and the dying light of evening, carefully observed and beautifully described in 'Evening Light': 'At this my eyes, hard pierced, seek out / the very edge of sky and land, at its / most distant, soft, and straight geometry.'[43]

After 'Evening Light' the poems revert to a more normal flow, but these four poems – 'Retirement', 'Driving Home from Basingstoke Crematorium', 'Knowing too much' and 'Evening Light' – offer something special to the contemplation of life's deepest anxieties and, for the Christian, most fundamental conclusions. Sight, understanding, knowing, compassion and love, without which birth into this world is but a shell of what God intends for his created beings. Incarnate, Christ is the ultimate example for us of what humankind is meant for, and as our lives ebb and flow and ease towards their mortal eclipse, it is these things that we want to express, affirming what we have spent our lives devoutly seeking, and holding firm to a loving and compassionate spirit; barriers shrink, dusk descends, and the light is eternally there, but for a space, beyond our sight.

This chapter ends not there but back with the direct connection with the incarnation and David's lovely poem 'Nine Lessons and Carols; A Theological View', which I quote in its entirety:

Nine Lessons and Carols;
A Theological View

Every Christmas I wish St John would come
and read the final lesson for himself.
Then I could listen for his run of syllables;
his subtle language, the changes solved.

I'd hear his tone of voice; watch his eyes,
anything that could expose reality
and help the statutory feasting time
of Christmas, unfold more naturally.

I might, seeing him there, understand this word,
who is the Word. How it might mean something
that cuts as deep as any sword; yet
is the source of life, life's truth, its meaning.

And would John be surprised
by the words St Matthew wrote and set beside
John's Greek: words we know quite well
like stable, baby, straw, and star,
none of which St John had wish to spell.

So we are left to wonder in the annual rush,
whether one can be resolved into the other,
all swaddled somehow into the hush of a manger:
with both light, and child, and mother.[44]

3

Crucifixion

Reflections on Craigie Aitchison's Paintings 4

See
 the cross, but:

> Q. What is the dog doing there?
> A. Oh!
>   howling beneath the bright cross
>   his master is shining from.[45]

The cover picture of *Piecing Together* is a reproduction of this painting. I have seen these paintings myself and they are unexpectedly small. Somehow I imagined a vast canvas and the two glowing figures of Christ and the dog, painted on the same level pretty well, standing out at a distance across a huge cathedral or gallery. The impression is of intimacy and light and love, and there is nothing suggestive of pain or sorrow. The diminutive size maintains this thought as much as the artwork itself.

In moving to the poems associated with the Passion, we are entering a vein of poetry that encompasses a great number of poems, but also descriptions and interpretations in Scott's theological works. Before doing so, there is the book specific to the subject, namely *An Anglo-Saxon Passion*, to examine. It is a work partially involving a degree of interpretation and imagination, but based firmly on '41 leaves of stout vellum', containing prayers scribed 'in the year AD 900'.[46] The interpretation and imagination brings David Scott to assume the presence of the nun's musings as she copies the prayers. The story as to how he found these prayers is related in the opening pages of this small hardback publication, which is a series of events so happily unfolding that the whole sequence of prayers and their translation assumed an even greater relevance, as if providentially revealed. However, two things impressed themselves upon his mind. First was the 'sheer hard work of the translation',[47] and second, he 'kept the nuns in mind, in order to keep my feet on the ground, to hold on to some sort of reality, and to the purpose behind all the searching for authorship. *Prayers are for praying*' (my italics).[48]

If anyone is interested in the whole amazing enterprise that David Scott undertook, then going to *An Anglo-Saxon Passion* is the way to satisfy that desire. I will add just one more quotation from its introduction. It is a longish one, but worth reading for its revelation of David's mindset as he travelled to the British Library to handle the actual manuscript that he was using a copy of for the translation. He has arrived at the Library and waits to see the manuscript. As he does so, he reveals his mind as he is asked why he wanted to see this particular manuscript:

> Good question, why did I want to see it? Why was the Birch Hampshire Record Society publication not enough? On reflection it was because it contained prayers to a God I worship, about the death and passion of a Lord I hold dear, and whose death I take to be significant not only for myself but for the whole world. I wanted to see it because some anonymous scribe had taken the immense trouble to copy these prayers into a volume, along with the passion narratives from St Mark, St Luke and St John, in a handwriting which I now know is called 'miniscules', and had illumined some of the letters, in not half so memorable a way as the Lindisfarne Gospels but very simply and at about the same time. I wanted to share in the immense pains taken to make these prayers available to men and women, most probably monks and nuns, to make their days leading up to

the remembrance of the death of Christ helpful, meaningful and penitential. I wanted to come alongside Christ in these significant last few days of his life. I didn't actually say any of that to the Museum staff.[49]

Laying down these quite reasonable, but not necessarily easily understood by the uncommitted, reasons for wanting to link not just a manuscript across the millennia but more intimately with the disciplined devotion of one age and another, creates a basis for looking more closely at the understanding that David Scott brings to what another generation may have termed the veneration of the cross. But their practice was far from theoretical; they lived with a love 'strong as death' the very days and hours that they spent in devout contemplation of Christ's sacrifice; his body broken, his blood spilt for humanity that he had so intimately embraced. Light and darkness are important here, as Scott points out in another of his works in discussing the poetry of Henry Vaughan, contemplating whether or not Vaughan imagined the light appearing in the darkness or the darkness as 'representative of the forces of chaos and anarchy, and disruption which were all around him in the events of his time'[50] (are they not in our own?), pressing in on, or 'swamping', the light.

With these and many other thoughts developing from them, David Scott analyses the life and devotion of a ninth-century nun of Winchester, of the Benedictine foundation of Nunnaminster. His feel for what is real and powerful in these prayers and what lies at their heart is summed up in the introduction to his translation and commentary on the prayers themselves. This is expressing not the theology of the classroom but the power of the spiritual engagement of Christ with the forces of evil. The focus is on the reality of this colossal and costly battle, and the intensity is highlighted over and over again by the physical effects of the crucifixion:

> The body of Jesus is the one thing that could not bypass human suffering and death. He could not turn into an angel,

or a ghost, and evade the sheer humanness of pain and humiliation. It is the body of Jesus to which these prayers direct their primary focus.[51]

There is much of love in Scott's commentary, and his reasoning is sound, as his reach for suitable quotations from the Song of Songs enhances the combination of powerful earthy prayer and deep spiritual reality. The reason for his attention to this manuscript is, overall, the same as his desire to hold the original in his hand. But as with the careful juxtaposition of the dog and our Lord in the Craigie Aitchison painting, driving its allegorical point home through the levelling of the height and size and the similar state of shining in a dark place, so the exploratory consideration of the wounds of Christ makes the link, not this time to the master/servant relationship but to the renewing effect of self-sacrifice.

Early in his collected poems, David Scott produces a form of George Herbert's poetic musings on the wounds throughout the Passion narratives from Herbert's Latin originals. These 'Excerpts from the Passion' appear in *Playing for England*.[52] I imagine these as I read as something of an academic exercise and their impression is descriptive and helpfully questioning (for example, 'Christ, hope of the whipped, victor of the world / when crimes multiply, and my punishment draws near / may your more gentle whip, the shadow of your whip suffice'). I can't help but compare these with some of the more personal, heartfelt references to the cross, with the referencing back to Good Friday in the three Easter poems published 16 years later in *Piecing Together*. Here is the mature priest walking through Winchester, 'feeling the weight / of the lowering of Christ, and smelling / the sacrificial hot-cross buns'. He asks himself a personal question that I doubt he would have asked a decade and a half before: 'Why am I so keen to stay with death / and sorrow, so cautious of the light, / and all that yellowness?' What, indeed, does he mean by 'all that yellowness'? He is not being implicit here, but surely in his mind he can see the stained cloth, the 'shrivelled vine', even on that first

CRUCIFIXION

Easter Day morning; he sees in the tomb; that 'Only clothes / remained, limp like a broken heart'. The 'piecing together' of the title of this collection is the miracle of the resurrection – but more of that in due course. The earthiness of these later reflections on the death of Christ and the impact that the Passion was having on him is direct, revealing and telling.

Let us look at a couple of late poems specifically referencing Christ's Passion. They are side by side in *Beyond the Drift*. The first – a reflection on another artwork by David Jones – is 'Crucifixion, 1926'.[53] This poem continues the earthy quality of Scott's feel for Christ's experience of suffering, but is also dependent for its interpretation on perspective. Each of the three short verses ends with the words 'as the cross rose higher and the sun sank down', though the first time they appear the order is changed to 'as the sun sank down and the cross rose higher'. The impression that the engraving and its subject matter together appears to be having – as the poem is constructed – is of a world that, as each day passes, is creating yet more reason to raise the cross of Christ, with the double meaning that the need for reconciliation in a world of mistaken ways of sin and failure is ever there, but also that the cross having become the symbol of that reconciliation, as well as the instrument of it, needs to be more and more visible. The first verse contains references to what has been, the second to the spiritual crisis on the first Good Friday, and the third to the ultimately passive and diminutive response of John and the women at the cross, as it 'rose higher and the sun sank down'. Comparing this poem to the next, namely 'Good Friday and the Magnolia Tree',[54] is creating a different sort of contrast. Every priest who has experienced preaching the Three Hours on Good Friday afternoon knows the dazzling light of stepping out of a church building into the sunshine of a 'normal' Friday afternoon, weekend approaching. 'I come out of church / smack into the full shopping sun' says it all. David relates seeing a young courting couple under a magnolia tree sharing 'the first ice cream of spring' and he knows that this is a contrast that he would not wish to change. This is 'down to earth' and goes with the contemplation of the reality that is expressed on the first Good Friday in the spitting, shouting, condemnation and scorn.

To understand David's devotional contemplation of the cross, we look particularly at the final chapter of his 2007 book on *The Mind of Christ*, that year's Mowbray Lent Book. The climax of the book and of the Passiontide end of Lent, the author focuses on 'Christ Minds: The St John Passion'. This title heads Chapter 10 of *The Mind of Christ*, and its beginning develops thoughts around light, Logos and eternal life, as we might expect. Scott demonstrates how the reader is eager to know more, and latches on to anything that illuminates the person of Jesus Christ that St John is so gloriously revealing. Indicating that we must view Good Friday through the lens of Maundy Thursday, he shows how what he calls the two sacraments revealed that night at the Last Supper are of crucial importance: the sacrament of the Eucharist, demonstrated in the sharing of bread and wine in that meal, and the sacrament of love demonstrated by Christ washing the feet of the disciples. The altercation with Peter over the disciple's objection to having his feet washed by his master serves to show that to be part with our Lord in his life and ministry means being united with him in his self-giving acts of love and acceptance. David says some important things at this point very directly:

> The sacrament of the Eucharist and the sacrament of love are two ways to the mystery of eternal life. Yet who wants eternal life? Have we not been too excited by the quick-fix rewards of this life, that we long for the rewards that are 'now', what *we* want? Looked at like that, eternal life seems boring by comparison. We are prepared to live for 'kicks' now and take our chance that the future will come to us anyway, without our asking, as part of the package of ordinary life – our rights, so to speak. But again, no. We have got to want eternal life and to want to spend our lives engaging in the desire for it and learning how that desire slips in between us and God's grace.[55]

CRUCIFIXION

Through this reasoning David Scott demonstrates that love for the one who offers eternal life to us is the secret, and that that love is in response to the love Christ shows for us. Referring to one of Baron von Hügel's letters to his niece[56] (he was her spiritual director and often they corresponded by letter – David mentions this in a poem), he reminds her of some thoughts they must have shared before as he approaches his own death:

> I wait for the breath of God. Perhaps he will call me today – tonight. Don't let us be niggardly towards God ... Plant yourself on foundations that are secure – God – Christ – Suffering – the Cross. They are secure. Caring is the greatest thing – my faith is not enough, it comes and goes – Keep your life a life of prayer, dearie – Keep it like that: it's the only thing, and remember; no joy without suffering – no patience without trial – no humility without humiliation – no life without death.[57]

These quotations, one from David Scott, the other from Friedrich von Hügel, are important as we read the long passages of reassurance in St John's Gospel that precede the arrest and crucifixion of Christ. David is assuming, as far as it is possible, the mind of our Lord as he approaches his death on the cross and what effect that death was going to have; critical to that understanding is the release of the Holy Spirit at the crucifixion itself. Now, most Christians would understand our Lord's words to the disciples at the Last Supper of the coming of the Comforter – when he leaves them, to prepare a place for them in John 14.2 and following – to mean after the ascension, and relate it directly to the descent of the Spirit on the disciples in the Upper Room on the Day of Pentecost, but what David Scott sees happening is 'The crucifixion released the Holy Spirit, the Comforter, to be the human Christ with us, freed from the limitations of the human body, but with the same powerful nature.'[58]

I believe that what he is describing here is less a chronological fact than a combination of conclusions that caused the outcome he describes. In this way his interest in Thomas Merton is relevant. In 2010 Scott preached a series of sermons for Good Friday in St Lawrence's, Winchester, which were later published. They appeared in the *Church Times* at the season of Passiontide following his death.[59] In these addresses he examines the theology of the cross of St Paul, Simone Weil and Thomas Merton. Each contains a perceptive core understanding. When it comes to Thomas Merton, particularly, one feels that Merton's theology and outlook is chiming with his own, though it is true that his feeling is for them all. He quotes Merton thus:

> If you want to have in your heart the affections and dispositions that were those of Christ on earth, consult not your own imagination, but faith. Enter into the darkness of interior renunciation, strip your soul of images and let Christ form himself in you by his cross.[60]

He goes on:

> What Merton felt, and ultimately felt in the heart of himself, was that he had been made new. It was the Spirit's work, the work of love, the Spirit of Christ. He described it like this: 'You keep finding this anonymous Accomplice burning within you, like a deep and peaceful fire.'
> He said: 'Life in Christ is life in the mystery of the Cross. We are involved in a sacrifice which brings struggle, but it also brings peace and a sense of rightness.'[61]

It seems that David Scott is drawing several crucially important thoughts together. The first is the concept of my being in Christ and Christ in me, being rooted absolutely in the cross. The second is that the death of Jesus on the first Good Friday didn't produce such a hiatus in spiritual renewal as we might imagine. In fact, from the moment of Christ's death the transforming nature of his Spirit released from the flesh was at work in the hearts and minds of his followers, including, let us not forget, Joseph of Arimathea and Nicodemus. The third point, related to it, is that this transformation is mysterious and, in Merton's words quoted above, 'burning like a deep and peaceful fire', but not easily pinned down, hence the thoughts of the Spirit as wind and fire and of undetectable direction. The fourth point is that experiencing this transformation ensures one is engaged in sacrifice. A further quotation from Scott's Good Friday address is needed here, referring to Thomas Merton once more:

> And he also says this about sacrifice, which comes fresh to my ears: 'The implication seems to be that sacrifice is something subjective and hard. The true notion of sacrifice is, on the contrary, something quite objective, and the note of difficulty or pain is not essential to it except in so far as our weak and fallen nature comes into conflict with the divine will.
>
> "By rights, there is no reason why a perfect sacrifice should not also be painless: a pure act of adoration, a hymn to the divine glory sung in ecstatic peace." That's original! That our sacrifices for one we love can be a joy, a matter of deepest love.'[62]

So it is that the release of the Spirit at the death of Christ into the lives of his followers can be seen with an immediacy and unpredictability, while experienced in fullness and with power and with corporate energizing and amazement on the Day of Pentecost. The gift of the Holy Spirit had already become a reality as the immediate band of our Lord's followers were being led to understand the implications of his resurrection, all this being interpreted as an unveiling of the power of self-giving within the small community that was to become the early Christian Church.

It is not surprising that the truths that Thomas Merton projected through his writings on to the hearts and minds of his readers were forged in silence and solitude. The mysteries of the Christian faith that are assumed in the regular receiving of Holy Communion, and in the expression of faith in prayer and action, are holding the features that David Scott contemplates through the writings of others on the cross, and especially through Merton. This by no means diminishes the imaginative thought that Scott brings to his own reflection on Scripture and his appreciation of the lives and direction of others. Returning to the poetry, there is a sequence of thoughts brought up in David's record of his visit to Skellig Michael that illustrates this very point.

Skellig Michael, since its use (some would say misuse) as a location for part of a *Star Wars* film, has become familiar, and its precipitous 670 steps and dry stone, ancient monastic buildings are recognized as a result. However, to physically reach it is essentially no easier, nor is its Christian site diminished historically. The 1994 etching of *Skellig Rocks, Co. Kerry* by Norman Ackroyd, which creates the atmospheric front cover of *Beyond the Drift*, forms a good backdrop to the poem 'Skellig Michael: A Pilgrimage', though the poem first appears in *Piecing Together*. This is essentially a penitential visit that responds to the awesome features that David and others have described on arrival at this place, where a community of monks clung to existence on an inhospitable rock in a frequently stormy Atlantic Ocean. The exact years of their tenancy at this place that has inspired writers, artists, pilgrims and naturalists cannot be known, but the approximate length of the occupation by a succession of monks was 700 years from its foundation in the sixth century. The community's beehive cells and other buildings are 230 metres above the sea, and the rocks lie some 12 kilometres of difficult sailing conditions off the south-west coast of Co. Kerry. The background information helps to appreciate why anyone chooses to go there and the impression they are left with having been.

It is not difficult to build on the outlook and theological wrestling of St Paul, Simone Weil and Thomas Merton to understand how David Scott is carrying the cross in a contemplative way. His capacity for quiet devotion is inclined

CRUCIFIXION

to draw us into a place of penitence and reflection on the condition of others, and hence in humility and sacrifice, yet involving something beyond us as well. David would say with Merton: 'our sacrifices for one we love can be a joy, a matter of deepest love'. Let us follow this through in the text of the poem as he steps ashore:

> ... you begin to hear the silence
> pressing in, far from the engine of the boat
> and the orchestrated scream of the gulls.
>
> Then the steps begin, the Southern Stairway,
> counting six hundred up to an unknown bedroom.
> Somehow it felt necessary to be discalced,
> my feet, white as a gannet's breast, my boots
> hanging round my neck like earrings.
> The boatmen I noticed, stayed below.
>
> Rightly, to enter the enclosure you have
> to stoop, awkwardly, lowly. You begin by bowing.
> In, you cannot see your way out.

A few lines later, we read:

>   Stop.
> Breathe. Let in the peace, and if you don't kneel there
> where on earth will you kneel?[63]

There is more, of course. The whole poem is full of mystery, about what we don't know, and how we can and are caught unaware, and the closeness of life to death, and the huge contrast between how an ordinary day in the office can be transformed, and:

> ... we'll take the boat again, and climb
> with the gulls willing us up further into lightness
> for which prayer is the only music, and Christ's coming
> the only purpose under heaven.[64]

Although the Norman Ackroyd engraving locates this poem in *Beyond the Drift*, and I am inclined to read it there, it does fit *Piecing Together*, where, as I mentioned earlier, it first appears. That locates it with other pilgrimage poems and the 'piecing together' of the resurrection that we shall contemplate later. Holding these thoughts in mind while reflecting on the crucifixion is helpful too, for everything is theologically connected, and David Scott is broad-minded in his understanding of the spiritual, as we would expect. The 'heart' is human and goes on pilgrimage with intent, desire and the need to search for truth and meaning. That does not lead everyone to Christ, much as the Christian may hope it would. 'Heart on Pilgrimage' is drawn

> to the foot of the cross,
> to the edge of the world,
> to the eye of the Buddha,
> the muezzin, the kestrel
> hovering over the motorway[65]

Yet attraction is something akin to faith, but of a different order, and the Church of the Holy Sepulchre as an actual place of pilgrimage rather than an idea or concept or generic object requires a deeper and more reflective poem:

The Church of the Holy Sepulchre, Jerusalem

> She is in love with someone, I can tell.
> When she sits, she sits alone and still.
> Her shrouded face, encompassing profound denials,
> surfaces in light, and says, 'I will'.
>
> Her movement speaks of shadows, edges,
> and who it is she loves is not found here,
> not there, but moving from the centre
> of her longing, is with her everywhere.[66]

CRUCIFIXION

Exploring the use of silence is a recurrent theme from Skellig Michael to the Church of the Holy Sepulchre and David links it with waiting, something he was very good at, peering into the depths of 'Qumran, Cave no. 4',[67] from which, by the chance discovery of a Bedouin boy, important Dead Sea Scrolls were discovered having lain unseen for two millennia. Through the chink between slats a woman watches men at prayer and wonders, her mind absorbed by possibilities that have yet to be realized in 'Mea Shearim, Jerusalem',[68] while a boat lies at anchor, dreamily watched in 'A Boat on Iona Bay'.[69] More obviously resting in quietness is 'The Friends' Meeting Room', which moves from the more obvious embarrassing silence as a break in conversation to the silence that brings one to one's knees in the still space of an ancient church. But most meaningfully, for this poem at least, is the cultivated quiet of the Quaker meeting:

in a room of many windows
and much light, is another silence
palpable, gathered by life's long haul
attempting to do the right thing,
silence waged with thought, and moral.[70]

'A Peculiar Clarity' brings us David's own need for silence and stillness, and ability to wait:

If I want to hold the silence
to its natural depth, I wait:
wait for the door to bang, the mower
to come to the end of its endless turning,
wait even for clothing to cease to rub
on clothing. Then I wait still more
until the way is clear for the bird
to sing its invisible song,
travelling a long way on the silence,
breaking nothing by its being heard.[71]

From these silences and waiting let us return to David's reflections on the Passion according to St John. We observe the authority of Christ in John's account and David directs us to consider two conversations, which are interwoven and create a scene of some importance. The drama takes place at the high priest's house; Annas is before the bound Jesus, while Peter is in conversation with those outside seeking warmth and light:

> Peter was in denial, refusing to acknowledge his discipleship of Jesus. Jesus at his religious trial was responding to questions about his teaching with the subtlest of answers ... Jesus had maintained a silent witness to truth. Peter denied all knowledge of the Lord and by his denial played false.[72]

The narrative in the Fourth Gospel continues as the scene changes to Pilate's headquarters, David Scott demonstrating that the few words spoken by Jesus and recorded by John are of great importance, as we see the time to keep silence and the time to speak are illustrated so significantly. In John 18.35, 36 we have words, that, as Scott points out, include those that were 'the most remarkable and explosive words of Jesus that have reverberated through time ever since'.[73] In reply to Pilate's questioning, Jesus says, 'My kingdom is not from this world.' Once more, we are directed to consider not the physical dimension of a place and power-base but the mystery that is faith in one who personifies a kingdom not of this world. Pilate and Jesus continue in dialogue about the nature of truth. Within all of this conversation is the awareness by John, being proclaimed to us, that while within this crucifixion narrative there is superficial recognition of the Passover custom of prisoner release, much more crucially there is the steady heartbeat of Christ's majesty declaring God's glory, and within the inner silence a great moment of truth and love was waiting to unfold.

Such a majestic and commanding understanding of the Passion is found among the Anglo-Saxon crosses, and upon one of these, in 'The Ruthwell Cross', Scott weaves some fine words:

The Ruthwell Cross

This Christ heads out to the Atlantic
and is battered by winds and weather.
Carved in majesty with simple strokes
nothing more subtle would have held together.

This is no delicate Christ.
This was set up to astonish,
and on this the gulls could
scan for fish, waves could crash.

Whoever carved this, knew
Christ in glory;
a match for the sun,
the hero of the story.

They set it in earth to
reach to the centre, up to
the heavens, across to the edges.
Within its spars were wrapped

the marvels of creation,
such that even the mystic
Magdalen, should share with
the Christ of the edgeless Atlantic.[74]

On the subject of crucifixion I have hung a number of thoughts that are not directly connected with the Passion of Christ, but I have tried to indicate, and use David's poetry and prose to declare, that essence of his thought and feelings around the mystery of Christ's self-giving, expressed only too often in a quiet and reflective way but at the same time with a focus that does not shy away from the reality of the powers of nature and human arrogance that challenge our need to express desire for God at every moment. The passing of natural life and the consciousness of historical events and the fleeting lives of human beings are all part of the transient experience of being a person of feeling and sensitivity, both emotionally and spiritually. The expression of the working of the Holy Spirit in the lives of the disciples of Jesus *from the moment of his death* is something that I hold dear from David's writings, as he found such encouragement from the view of Thomas Merton that 'there is no reason why a perfect sacrifice should not also be painless: a pure act of adoration, a hymn to the divine glory sung in ecstatic peace.'[75] This discovery is another for which I am grateful. Maybe it is that David is hinting at this thought by choosing to write a poem on 'Michelangelo's Rondanini Pietà'.[76] The incomplete final work of Michelangelo is not so much without pain as reflecting a deep and complete sadness. Is there peace? Is there adoration? I'm not sure. This is David's poem:

Michelangelo's Rondanini Pietà

It is all still being made
and it is all just breaking up.
He is being carried, and she
is carrying him now. He is bearing up,
and now is carrying her
in such an awkward verticality:
both so tired, so sad. His work
is done: hers, now over, begins again.
The only hope lies in the spring of
knees, which are broken, but ready
for resurrection. The whole world
is on his back, crying 'now!'

Moving from the crucifixion to the resurrection, I use another of David's poems to provide a gentle and reflective transition:

CRUCIFIXION

St Herbert's Isle, Derwentwater

Island of the wild garlic
Island of the brooding geese
Island of the fallen oaks
Island of the birds in chorus
    of the lapping water
    of the sun on my page

Island of the mossy shore
Island of the stone pillow
Island of the spiritual friend
Island of the British trees
    of the roots above ground
    of the spider on my page
    of the manuscript heads of ducks

Island without ice cream
Island without notices
Island to kiss the ground of
Island to make decisions in
Island of the geese trumpeters
    of the beetle on the leaf mountain

        where oak trees grow out of oak trees
        where Bede is still read

        soft island, safe island,
        Island where you've not seen it on a bad day

        St Herbert pray for us
        St Cuthbert pray for us
        the author of the 'Anonymous
        Life of Cuthbert' pray for us

        Not that it was easy for them.
        It brought Herbert to the bone of endurance.

BE STILL, BE SILENT

Island of the ministry of angels
Island of the lonely death
Island of a glorious resurrection.[77]

4

Resurrection

Resurrection

I think it took her death to do it.
The light that emanated from the space
she left spoke resurrection.
Who she was took hold of time
and turned it inside out,
and the old laughter which took
such toll of pompous hats and dirgy hymns
was transfigured into something
which got under the skin of suffering
and put it in its place.

So now I tell the secret
that resurrection is the glass
through which we see things differently,
and what was first in the mind of God
becomes the truth at last.[78]

This is a fascinating poem for it demonstrates David Scott's ability to bring the resurrection of Christ to a point of a looking, a space, a lens, a movement, rather than a point in time, a moment of miracle. Then light of the resurrection spoke from a space left by someone who had died. Now we could draw conclusions from this idea if used to illuminate what was happening on that first Easter Day at the tomb in the garden being visited by Mary Magdalene and the other women, to anoint the body of Jesus. Of course, Mary Magdalene didn't see everything as it was, for she looked at Jesus but saw a gardener. She could only fully see when she understood the truth that the resurrection proclaimed as the lens through which one saw reality in its fullness and depth. We may add the disciples' unseeing meeting with Jesus on the Emmaus road to the unrecognized 'gardener' of that morning at the tomb.

David Scott comments:

> One of the strongest, though what might be considered one of the weakest, features of the resurrection is the gentleness with which Christ returns. We might think the resurrection would have deserved more of a flourish, trumpets and a brass band at least, but Christ returns with peace, assurance, comfort ...[79]

In its broadest sense, 'this peacefulness that is so persuasive'[80] is present in other Scott poems that are not ostensibly about the resurrection at all. Taking *Piecing Together* as the most directly theological of his collections, there are, of course the three Easter poems – (*I*), (*II*) and (*III*)[81] – all of which draw significantly on Good Friday and look at the crucifixion through the lens of Easter morning, as we might expect. *Easter I* uses the metaphor of a physical lifting to bring an ongoing knowledge of forgiveness to parallel faith in the resurrection. David puts it much better in the poem, but silence and grace come together with the song of the thrush chiming '*unique ... unique ... unique*', providing the closing words that are not words but birdsong that is peacefulness. *Easter II* takes the annual return of spring as a reminder of the new rather than its creator. Once again Easter Day is a window through which Christ is stretched, 'hanging on the axle-tree, / nailed to the east and the west / ... love all alive on the sudden'. *Easter III* likens the empty tomb to 'a mouth aghast, / all presence gone and so fast'. Yet there is birdsong once more, this time sparrows and larks; but that birdsong only inspired the music, the tune, to which he had earlier been deaf. This third Easter poem is the more heartfelt, closing with the words, 'The tomb was empty but my heart was full. / Love pieced together Christ and made him whole.'

There is surely a play on 'pierced' and 'pieced' in David's mind. Christ as the personification of the Love of God is pierced (that is, nailed to the cross) for love of humankind; for the broken and the fallen; the sinful and the failure; the lost and the dying. Restitution, resurrection, renewal. A making whole. A piecing together.

Always there is the gentle observation of the incidental, the sparrow, lark or thrush, the green hill, the cockerel's crimson throat, the purple pillar, as St John noted in his Gospel account, the time of day, the weather, the exact place. In *The Mind of Christ*, David makes the point that 'Christ makes every attempt to remove fear and replace it with faith.'[82] Thinking through the resurrection appearances of Jesus one can see this in each scene, but David also relates it as part of the gentleness and peace, lack of condemnation and constant appeal to the disciples in such a way as to open their eyes. This appears as an essential element of the pastoral gift of the priest, taking for example 'Scattering Ashes' in *A Quiet Gathering*.[83] Many clergy have been called to do what they may wish to perform otherwise, but, within reason, will attempt to fulfil what they know will be the most loving thing. But it is not just kindness, it is a way of making Christ known to those for whom he is a stranger; of expressing the faith of the Church through the ministry of compassion. In this the priest is the instrument, and prays for the words, and way of saying them, that will bring the reality of the faith professed to the piecing together of the pierced; the desire to make whole the broken-hearted.

'The Funeral'[84] of the poet William Scammell, who died at the age of 61 in the year 2000, reflects another such occasion for David. In this poem the relationship of the church building to the man to be buried from it is sensitively put. In fact, the balance of the whole poem is just right for the sentiments it expresses. There is a teasing out of that commonly held belief that the church building should be there and yet the need to enter it is not, nor has it been, until this time of departure.

BE STILL, BE SILENT

David has been asked to speak, conduct the service and be the one to 'have the final word'. But it is a static finale, with a 'sleeping church', a 'comforting and clumsy ritual', a place to gather, to wonder, to reminisce, but those words, 'without you', at the end are poignant and sad.

It is 'Flower Rota',[85] another poem in this general theme of loss, that has stood over the years as one of David's poems that I have particularly loved. It is because I have known many women, and I think they have all been women, whose service to the church in being part of the flower rota is a gift, yes, but also a mark of love. There is much not said in this poem. In fact its beauty lies in the hinted-at but not spoken; the action that holds both words and tears. Again the incidental details add something that makes the whole poem come alive with resonating life: the pen that runs out that has sat long in a damp church, the presence of the Visitors' Book, the noticeboard, the chicken wire.

There is sadness in all of these poems, but they breathe a life that is lived beyond the superficial, and beyond this one. One could argue that it is simply feeling part of the historical continuity of a community, but for the Christian, with the events surrounding the resurrection of our Lord in mind, there is so much more. The desire to overcome fear and failure is an emotional response that David is exploring, among other feelings, viewed from a standpoint of faith. Small actions are divining deep emotions, reacting on the human love that is drawn from its divine origin. *Piecing Together* ends with a poem that illustrates what I am trying to tease out, that, in David's mind and heart, there is something (yes, creative, because he is a poet) that is tugging at him, that he can't always put down in pen on paper. It is, I believe, St Augustine's restlessness, ever searching, desiring that eternal life that is the gift of God in Christ Jesus. David wrote that it is not enough just to expect it to happen, we have to desire it, as I quoted above from *The Mind of Christ*: 'We have got to want eternal life and to want to spend our lives engaging in the desire for it and learning how that desire slips in between us and God's grace.'

RESURRECTION

It may be that the urge to write poetically and be imaginative and seek metaphors for anything that is somehow incomplete and not tied down overlaps with this desire, but perhaps that too is natural. I recall hearing Canon John Fenton, about whom David has written a poem (mentioned in Chapter 1), speaking at a clergy meeting in Winchester saying that trying to understand St John's Gospel is like looking at a lorry with a tarpaulin covering its load. There is always a bit that is loose and flapping in the wind – not his exact words of course, but that's how I remember it. With 'Written in Juice of Lemon'[86] we feel the writer's need to smooth things out within and express the perfection of what he is trying to explain, but who is that comforting someone if not the Holy Spirit?

Written in Juice of Lemon

Some poems I write in ink
and they get written with a lot
of furrowing of the brow, and often miss
but some I write in juice of lemon
quickly in my heart
and hope that one day someone's
warmth will iron the secrets into poems
with effortless art.

The experience of the Christian in being 'in Christ' and inspired with his Spirit is one that has received and will receive many and varied testimonies. The resurrection of our Lord recalibrated the disciples in a way that the New Testament is our window into understanding. The transformation was, in the case of his closest followers, both men and women, achieved at least most obviously by the physical reappearance of Christ on the first Easter Day and in the 40 days that followed. David Scott, understandably, places considerable importance on how the mishmash of emotions and questions was ironed out:

The greeting with which Christ returned from the dead was 'Peace be with you!' There was nothing ghoulish or over-dramatic about his return. He came to calm, to allay fears, not to excite. The atmosphere in which Jesus had his encounters with others is subsumed in a sense of awe and tranquillity. The brief statements breathe confidence and a gentle authority. They even overlap and apparently conflict: 'Do not hold on to me,' (Jn 20.17) says Jesus to Mary Magdalene, and 'Put your finger here' (Jn 20.27) to Thomas. He came to strengthen faith and reduce fear and for each he seemed to have a personal message.[87]

The resurrection accounts in the Gospels, the pastoral ministry of a priest, the poetic reflections on emotional and spiritual experience, the practice of prayer and the passing of time coalesce, whether we are wary of drawing these threads together or not. Scott writes of the importance of Scripture in forming the mind, or perhaps, better still, in texts 'dropping into us, into the rich and fertile soil of a listening receiving soul', with the example of the parable of the sower.[88] What we are shimmying around here is the inclination of poetry, written from a faith perspective, not only to illuminate theological truths but at least to be partially responsible for defining them. The resurrection accounts are particularly susceptible to this kind of interpretation. David Scott gives us this important passage:

> S. T. Coleridge (1772–1834), the poet and religious philosopher, talked about the difference between 'fantasy' and 'imagination', and I think it is a helpful distinction to draw with our approach to Bible reading. Fantasy takes images and excites the mind in ways so removed from reality that it builds up a frustration and anxiety when they are not realized. The imagination, Coleridge said, is the creative thought process which is able to transform pictures and images into realistic routes for charting a way forward. Again, the art analogy helps. The artist takes material that is reasonably

familiar to most people and makes new, unique patterns out of it. That creative process can be used with our reading of Scripture. The building blocks of Scripture are reasonably familiar, but our imaginations can reassemble them in unique ways in order to let God speak and act through us for our time.[89]

While fully aware of the dangers of redefining Christian belief through poetry used at some funerals and other liturgical celebrations, Scripture itself is full of poetic explanations of the relationship between God and humanity, and indeed relationships of faith that are part of the warp and weft of human existence and so vital to the priest/poet's art. Acknowledging the dangers is something I am certain David Scott would have been ever conscious of. But not only did he pen tender and beautiful expressions of Christian understanding, he treasured those given to him by others. I think that this awareness is especially demonstrated in 'Just a Line'[90] with his sincere gratitude to a few words from the poet Geoffrey Holloway.

Just a line
(for Geoffrey Holloway)

It happened
having just cracked the spine
that my eye
and mind found the perfect
converting line.
Before was never
the same as after.
The line will go with me
to the grave, perhaps
see me through it.

It was something to do with
a swimming pool
and the feeling of trust
between swimmer
and water, father
and daughter.

I had felt it
and you had said it,

poet.

The landscape of the west of Ireland seems to lend itself to reflection on life and death, and has been and still is the home of artists, writers, poets and naturalists – as well as those who carry out the normal occupations that maintain the fabric of society! We have noted already that from the southwest David visited Skellig Michael, but the whole area from Donegal to Dingle is extraordinarily touched with the wide vistas and sparse population of the dramatic and sometimes frankly frightening sweep of the Atlantic seaboard. David's poems from this area sense the spiritual consciousness of the place, and while 'For Martin'[91] is imagining the thorns on Christ's crown on the cross, as he contemplates the miles of gorse in the countryside, it is with a sense of renewal and life. Gorse has both thorn and rich flower. This contrast is exposed in the poem:

For Martin

Strange how gorse
has thorn and rich flower
both – all along
the hills and roadsides
from Carrowkeel to Portsalon
and on the slopes of Murren.

RESURRECTION

> My Saviour caught his coat
> on gorse. Fingering
> the torn cloth and trammelled thread
> he spoke of death being
> thorn and rich flower
> both.[92]

All of these are examples of how the poetry that has been written and continues to be written illuminate the Christian faith, and it is as a priest that David Scott is expressing his utterly convinced belief in the resurrection of Christ:

> The New Testament was inspired by the resurrection of Jesus Christ. It was at that point that literature was uniquely put at the disposal of faith. We treasure its heritage in the Old Testament, for those roots go very deep and feed the New Testament. At points they are inextricable, but the real driving force of the New Testament is the raising of Christ from the dead, defeating the old enemy, death, and opening out hope to all who have faith in the power of Christ Jesus to save.[93]

David, throughout his life as a poet, put his writing 'at the disposal of faith', and though at times it is assumed and not overt it is there, with resurrection, new life, renewal, and the fact that death is not the end essential to the understanding of numerous poems.

An Afternoon Walk

> I've been following wild garlic
> round all my life, on river banks,
> with the river deepening its bed
> lifting up the sandstone layers,
>   and with the falling the rising
>   and with the rising the deepening.

BE STILL, BE SILENT

And are the celandines both yellow
and white in among the nettles?
And is that blossom on the ground
just two heads? Take me to the
tree you came from just now
your stamen freckled blossom,
your bees' food.

I might have expected the blossom
but not this welcome. Such
a crowded beauty, a bee
might not know where to begin.
Even the trunk leans with its
lightweight load, blushing
against the dark yew of the churchyard
backed by hill upon hill.

In the empty church,
the patient mechanism
of the clock, ticks

    back,
    forth,

    back,
    forth

    back ...[94]

Afterword

Nothing was ever going to entirely fit a structure imposed upon a body of poetry, and placing four major Christian themes as chapter headings, though drawing on many of David Scott's poems, I was always going to leave out some delightful and often very touching or humorous pieces that I cannot finish without mentioning, even if I can't do them justice.

I am starting with a poem that didn't make the cut for *Beyond the Drift*: it is the Betjemanesque 'Autumn in Wivelrod', which appears only in *Piecing Together*. I mention it because, apart from liking its mild teasing, Wivelrod was part of my parish when I served in Winchester Diocese and I can picture the scene so well.

Autumn in Wivelrod

When talk's of harvest and of God
then autumn's come to Wivelrod.
The blackberry pips lodge in the teeth,
the ferns are wilting in the heat.
The summer's fiercest sun appears,
so that confirms that autumn's here.
O shining, chestnut thoroughbred,
twitching for the mistress-head.
She's gone to school with trunk and rug,
which means, it's Christmas for the hug.
She'll share her dreams with you, and O,
the boy who shared the pedalo.

The lonely biplane in the sky
drones to wish the bees goodbye.
The football shirts are on the line.
The team is back for one more time.
The acorns drop, the beech nuts fall,
I didn't need my coat at all.
I see the brown creeps up the leaf.
I sense an ancient form of grief.[95]

Following that little piece of nostalgia and indulgence, I shall run through David's five volumes of poetry and pick from here and there to complete this short study of the deep and quiet stream of poetry that has brought me back to its source many times, and will again.

A *Quiet Gathering* begins with 'Kirkwall Auction Mart', the poem that won David the *Sunday Times*/BBC national poetry competition in 1978. This volume of just 79 pages contains fine drawings by Graham Arnold that are more than just incidental to the book, but are memorable on their own. Together with the poems they create a collection that set a marker for what was to follow. I have quoted these poems less than any of the other collections largely because they haven't illustrated my main themes, which in a way is not surprising as I was seeking David Scott's most mature thought. But, naturally, they contain some lovely fresh, youthful poems that I read with a smile, and to which I shall return again and again. 'Cycling Holiday' is a case in point (is it David and Miggy, or just imagination?):

Cycling Holiday

They prop up the tandem outside the shop,
exchange toffees, slot cards for the parents
into the wall. The wind is fresh
and tugs at the map where tanned fingers
trace the next stretch: lunch

safe in the panier. The shop bell
rings out a regular customer; and they are set
ready on the pedals. But just a moment
while he scratches his bare knee
and she rearranges her pony tail.[96]

David had a wonderful eye for natural form, and several poems in this first collection illustrate that quality of observation that is spun out poetically. The form of a Lombardy poplar leaf and stalk are such that the wind can 'whisper its rumour', that of ash 'being pinnate / it will couple perfectly'.[97] Lough Derryduff, now beside a wind farm, sounds like a location for a child's Donegal holiday. A day fishing and walking over muddy terrain, one feels the tiredness but the desire to be alone in thought too, as 'liquid lights tremble in deep crofts', finger tracing the hills 'still / thick with condensation from the dog's breathing'.[98]

There is nostalgia of an almost forgotten form, except those of long memory and a literary mind trained in the writers of the inter-war years. The 1920s and '30s have a frozen-in-time quality that saw change on a prodigious scale, and '*Old English Household Life* by Gertrude Jekyll, 1925' is a time capsule that David unties in a few apposite words:

Old English Household Life by Gertrude Jekyll, 1925

Nostalgia was just browning up
especially with regard to household things
in West Surrey when Gertrude Jekyll wrote.
Museums were typing out the labels
with a black typewriter's huge letters:
dog turnspit, smock, pepper pot.
Even then we were being removed from dirt
and the patient keeping in of lights and fires.
The brasses, no more catching the sun,

came off the sweating foreheads of the horses,
onto the pub wall. Lych-gates no longer
rested the dead on the final walk up the path.
Each chapter heading was an epitaph.[99]

This lovely poem is followed by a run of weather-beaten verses that hold us in their atmosphere as we rest in comfort and incline our thoughts to less easy-going times: 'Rain', 'Mist', 'Herdwick', 'Curlew', 'Border Ballad' and 'Flanking Sheep in Mosedale' follow one another.[100] David is still referencing weather in the next poem, which I would like to quote in its entirety. There is no surprise that David read Ruskin, whose acute observations and descriptions from art to architecture would have enthralled him:

Ruskin's *Sketches from Nature*

There is a hurry in his sketch. The cloud
will only stay a while like that
before a serious change obliterates.
A cloud will not stay quiet: it burns
and draws in all that is around,
cusping and reeling across the Old Man of Coniston.
On his desk are the practice wads
of cotton, and the books to verify
what a cloud is. He delights to find
that clouds do not grow, but are sculpted down
by the warm air around, like masons
working on Venetian stone. How difficult
to get them down on paper.
So many sacks of flour. Except for Turner
the master of the cloud, who in his vignettes
and storm studies seemed to get them right.[101]

AFTERWORD

Leaving *A Quiet Gathering*, I move on to *Playing for England*,[102] the title poem of which is full of that delicious contrast that sees the qualities of England in a few of its various guises seem what one hopes they will ever hold: solid worth, shared traditions, understated but not undervalued hopes and dreams, and so on. This second collection, published in 1989, holds many of my favourite Scott poems. The last of these is an extraordinary poem when one thinks of the subject, but very funny and not to be sniffed at!

The Closure of the Cold Research Institute

Was it at Berkhamsted or Tring?
Well, anyway, it's just packed in.
Boffins' heads like Friedrich Nietzsche's
are seen emerging from the Chiltern beeches.
Olitsky and Macartney with files untold
have failed to trap the common cold.
We've got the hang of the other species,
we can tell which are the foreign cheeses.
Most common things we understand:
sparrows, cormorants, Prayers, and land,
but colds defy the common wit.
You get them, and that's it.
So that's it too for volunteers
and bottles labelled over many years;
tons of bumph and Government Issue
pulped into rolls of lime green tissue.
Still the nation's noses run
impervious to tots of rum.
The mother's eagerness to wipe
is countered by the child's swipe.
The dreadful sweat of boardroom meetings,
the midnight shakes, the fitful sleeping,
days off school, off work, off life,
the 'don't come near me's' of the wife,

all these presumes a fierce defiance
of man's experimental science.
We cannot check the flow of phlegm
or staunch the faulting speaker's 'hem'.
So if there are no more suggestions,
we'll have to be content with questions:
Which of the primates had it first?
Which of the Royal's had it worst?
If God intended it for man
what exactly was his plan?[103]

Piecing Together is David's most overtly theological collection, with a number of poems directly related to the cross. But there are others that hint at or tangentially approach a spiritual theme, which is always related in some way to the touchstone of Christ. Perhaps this is not obvious to those not looking for it, but as a priest reading the words and anticipating the thoughts of another priest I am never left with that feeling I sometimes have with other writers on a Christian theme they are not living – that it is academic and cold. With David, one is connecting as one reads his words with the heart and soul of the Christian priest who has moulded those words after living with them for a long time and prayerfully too. A good example of this is an early poem in *Piecing Together* called 'This Meadow, a Soul'.[104] This could be taken in a pluralistic way, even pantheistic, but the secrets lie in the references to the Scriptures and especially the Gospels. David's immersion in their events and incidental detail reveal what cannot be hidden, that Christ walked this land, his disciples handled and nibbled the seed heads, the breath of God sweeps across the face of creation, and we feel its effect on our faces, unseen but known through its mysterious presence. The souls of men and women are not picked apart as they live but, as in the parable of the weeds in the field, the farmer isn't always going to look at them and judge what is good seed and what is weed; the confidence is simply there that all will be well. I'm not saying that David Scott consciously thought all of this through as he penned his poem; it is just that it was going to be within him, as part of his Christian awareness.

Not scriptural this time but historical and factual is 'Caedmon's Song'.[105] Caedmon (c.658–80) is credited with producing the first hymn in English. A Northumbrian monk, he managed the animals for the community in Hilda's Whitby. David feels his day begin:

> Among the cattle, the air
> in the silence, the wind
> in the dust, I heard you
> before breakfast, and made
>
> this song of it.

Once more, the rooting of the poem in the Christian tradition is understated but ever present. Lest I give the impression that David was only interested in the teaching of Christianity and didn't see the common threads of humanity and its strivings for peace and justice, and aspirations for life in its holistic fulness in other faiths, then let us consider the poem 'Ibn Abbad woke early'.[106] In this poem Scott imaginatively brings a highly regarded fourteenth-century Islamic scholar and an eighteenth-century rabbi, well known in his day, to Fr Louis (aka Thomas Merton), and they talk freely. There is no argument as to who is right and who is wrong. The boy Jesus joins their hands and then disappears, to continue his work of bringing people together elsewhere:

> and that goes on today
> unceasing in his care to see beyond the robes
> of different length, and hue, and cloth,
> the common beating heart, and to mark again
> as on the Bethlem night, the angels' call:
> *Peace on the earth, good will to all, to all.*

But I finish this Afterword on *Piecing Together* with David's contemplation of the Gertrude Jekyll-designed garden on Lindisfarne, on the site of the castle's vegetable gardens. This poem contains a number of elements: a quotation from the Song of Songs, an admission of surprise that the planting is more common than he anticipated, the solid worth of seat and sundial, and the constants of sea, Cuthbert and the 'whole wide bowl of sky'.[107] It is a comforting poem full of happy memory; though perhaps not the greatest of David's poems, it holds its place for sheer joy.

In all three collections not containing selected poems from earlier full publications – *A Quiet Gathering*, *Playing for England* and *Piecing Together* – there are other poems that I pass over reluctantly and conscious of making subjective choices. *Selected Poems* appeared in 1998 – that is, before *Piecing Together* – and included 52 new poems, which do not appear again until *Beyond the Drift*. They begin with some nostalgic early memories, 'The Deserted Barracks' being the most piercing and taut with an inner recall of feelings that were best forgotten:

> ... a walking
> through the ruins of my childhood,
> knowing I can tread on them, and keep my
> head in the sun, and walk away from it for good.[108]

'Cleaning the Shoes'[109] is one of a number that David wrote that extol the virtues of simple, routine, manual tasks that engender reflection and relaxation. The incidental, the passing, the distraction, in fact the gentle occupation from singing to brushing a shoe, to observation of patterns on a wall, the polish on a step, the lines on a badminton court, name what you will; the observable intricacies of daily life are all important in connecting us with our past and with those with whom we seek to empathize.

There are several poems that relate to artists, saints and poets, but it is to 'Selborne, some 29th of Junes' that I am drawn

AFTERWORD

for its various associations of location and scope.[110] Selborne is a few miles from Winchester and not far from Wivelrod and the parish in which I served. It is the place made famous by Gilbert White, an extraordinary eighteenth-century naturalist and priest, whose record of nature and garden observations is among the most important publications on the subject for its time. The poem touches on the famous tulip tree, the beautiful gardens and the insect and bird life of the whole extended estate of *The Wakes*, Gilbert White's house with the garden, which is, in fact, more relevant than the house. It is a reminder of how these have been preserved as a backdrop for those who read the book, *The Natural History of Selborne*,[111] and admire the descriptions and understanding of Gilbert White. It is still read avidly today. Presumably David Scott, and perhaps his family too, visited on more than one 29 June, or it may reference the late June appearance of the damsel and dragon flies, and then the high-summer descriptions of more than one year are assimilated in the lines of the poem. All is observed as 'Dragon-flies', 'move like an architect's / rule', 'helicopt the pond' and 'come out of their amelia-state'. It is dream-like, raising up the 'saint of the close look, / staying put, notebook'.

A different reason draws me to a poem a few pages further on, still on what has passed but setting up contrasts. This is the reflective 'Between'.[112] David is standing leaning on a rusty railing at a harbour edge. It is a place of cliffs and hill, shadowed into ridges. His eye is moving from the small boats bobbing below him to the storm-thrashed heights in the distance. But at the same time the 'between' is referencing the time passing from what has been to what now exists. It is a poetic expression of what many may feel as one age is glimpsed through another and one perspective taken in while drawn to another.

There is movement observed by David in several poems in different ways, but all beautiful. 'Acrobatic swallows zim it / from wire to eave' appears in the short verse 'Dusk'[113] in the *Selected Poems*; while 'three girls / slip their links of iron, and

/ move in sacred space like dancers', in 'Abbey Ruins',[114] and St Francis of Assisi 'stood upside down, / rolled in the snow, for / forty days fasted on this island, / eating only the bread of the gospels', in 'A Postcard from Lake Trasimene'.[115] But the collection ends with a stop, approaching an abandonment, in 'My Bike'.[116] Visiting on a bicycle has the problem of arriving and not being quite sure how to leave the machine, while the 'talk ranges / from the now, to the past, to the weather / mostly skirting eternity', but once home the bike is left, 'like a laid hedge, / among bits of hose, tired footballs, / the rusty sledge. It sleeps where it falls.'

Following *Piecing Together*, it was another nine years before more new poems appeared at the end of *Beyond the Drift*. There are a number of new poems in the collection that refer to church buildings and their effect both in stirring spiritual or, perhaps better, ecclesiastical musings, as well as those that touch on one of David's frequent themes, meditating on those who have occupied this space before him, maybe long before. So we have 'Bowes Churchyard, Early Morning',[117] with thoughts about the incumbent's devastation at the death of his children, while a 'sparrow wheeled from headstone to headstone / cutting through the morning sun', and:

> The dustbin men had left the engine running.
> The emptying of bins, chugs and clumps
> and slams beside the churchyard wall,
> blocking any passing sentiment.

'Allhallows Church'[118] is subtitled '*A Dream*' and takes us into that realm of imagination that peoples a church building in more than one guise, but links both present celebration and past regular and lifetime worshippers. They are connected with singing and with the communion bread and 'all light and shining / in the latticed sun'. 'The Lanercost Poems'[119] follow, a sequence written in 2006 to mark the seven hundredth anniversary of the stay of Edward I at Lanercost Priory in 1306, also commemorated by the visit of Prince Edward to the site

AFTERWORD

in 2006. But it is in 'Tintern Abbey'[120] and 'Astley Church'[121] that I find the effect of visiting a church especially telling. In the latter, David mentions Philip Larkin's feeling on passing through the door recorded in his slightly dismissive, slightly questioning, slightly awe-filled and rather sad poem 'Church Going'. David leaves the door 'ajar', while Larkin lets it 'thud shut',[122] but it amounts to the same thing; neither actually shutting out the world beyond. In both of David's poems is the sense that peace should reign here, and light and rest; the pace of visiting should be slow, 'heel going gently down before the toe', and 'not to be concerned / about anything very much at all' (both quotations from 'Tintern Abbey'). I end in Astley, with David musing, 'I love the summer stillness of this Church' and leaving it 'exerts in me a mild shock of sun, / but steadied, I drift towards a poet's grave'. However, at this moment, surely he is reaching out 'beyond the drift', recalling but not singing Frances Havergal's exquisite words:

Take my life, and let it be
consecrated, Lord, to thee;
    take my moments and my days,
    let them flow in ceaseless praise.

Take my hands, and let them move
at the impulse of thy love;
    take my feet, and let them be
    swift and beautiful for thee.

Take my voice, and let me sing
always, only, for my king;
    take my intellect and use
    every power as thou shalt choose.

Take my will, and make it thine;
it shall be no longer mine;
    take my heart, it is thine own;
    it shall be thy royal throne.

BE STILL, BE SILENT

Take my love; my Lord, I pour
at thy feet its treasure store:
   take myself, and I will be
   ever, only, all for thee.[123]

Epilogue

The first David Scott Lecture

Given by Mark Oakley, then Chancellor of St Paul's Cathedral, Dean of Southwark since 2023. The lecture was first given at St Lawrence's Church, Winchester, on 25 November 2017.

Bishops of the Church of England are not always known for their poetic talents. However, one bishop of London, Henry Montgomery Campbell, who was known, among other things, for his dry humour did once try his hand at poetry. He wrote a short poem in his will and asked that it be read out to all of his clergy on his death. It simply said: 'Tell my priests when I am gone, o'er me to shed no tears; for I shall be no deader then, than they have been for years.'

Well, I cannot properly tell you how honoured I am to be asked to give this talk today in honour of David Scott. David obviously never worked for Bishop Montgomery Campbell because David is a priest very much alive to the world, to perception, to the numinous. Like all good poets he is one of the world's antennae and, like so many in this church today, I have admired both his work and his humanity for many years. To be here to celebrate both of these is a real joy for me and I am very grateful to be standing here.

Earlier this year I had the pleasure too of being part of the R. S. Thomas Festival, held in Aberdaron where Thomas had served as the vicar. It was a weekend of Thomas tribute, an R. S.-fest, where every aspect of the great priest-poet was explored. Again I was delighted to be asked to give a talk – that delight completely fizzled however when I was told I was following Rowan Williams. 'That's quite a warm-up act you've got there', said one wag. And of course, the former Archbishop of Canterbury stood up and gave a talk that said everything that needed to be said and without one note in front of him. By the time the Q and A arrived, I was busily trying to work out how to get out of my gig to save face – a migraine perhaps? A stomach bug of projectile proportions might do it.

But then someone asked a question that distracted me. A woman asked Rowan what R. S. had been like as a preacher. Rowan said he had never had the fortune of hearing him preach and couldn't really comment. A man at the back suddenly said: 'Oh! Elsie here was in his congregation, she'll know!' All eyes turned to the elderly Elsie in silent anticipation, as wisdom from Delphi was about to be received. 'You heard R. S. preach?' asked Rowan. 'Oh, yes I did,' she said. 'Often?' 'Oh yes, every Sunday for 12 years.' 'And, what was he like?' Rowan said on behalf of us all, now at the end of our seats. 'Oh!', she said, 'Dire!'

Every priest in that room heaved a private sigh of relief. Thank goodness. He was bad at something at last! R. S. Thomas of course was one of many British poet-priests. George Herbert, John Donne, Manley Hopkins, Robert Herrick, Robert Southwell and in our own day Rowan Williams, Malcolm Guite, Rachel Mann and, of course, David Scott. What is it I wonder that draws many clergy to the language of poetry? That question, in tribute to David, might be one way in to this day together because, although many of you aren't clergy, or if you are you are hiding it well, there may be converging resonances for us.

Not all clergy, of course, are naturally drawn to a poetic shaping of language. I once saw a very large billboard outside a north London church where the vicar was trying to entice shoppers with the message rather un-poetically: 'Tired of sin? Then come in.' To which someone had scribbled at the bottom 'But if not telephone 263635'. However, many clergy are drawn to poetry and I have one or two reflections as to why this might be. See what you think.

EPILOGUE

The former Dean of St Paul's, John Donne, said that the effectiveness of a preacher lay not in their wit or their cleverness or their authority. The effectiveness of a preacher lay, he said, in their 'nearenesse', how near, how close, they felt to those who were listening.[124] Was this a human being like them? The parish priest, like David, lives among his or her people, leading a congregation, yes, but also befriending a wider community, a locality, being there when, say, there is a tragedy as well as being there for people when they lose someone, love someone, celebrate a new life and so on. This nearness, being in tune with the realities of human lives, of the complexities of shared living and of the environments, political currents and events that affect us day to day for good or not, this nearness leads often to an inner need to be able to distil from time to time, to withdraw from the noise of now, to be able to read between lines, to distrust the first impression, to see where social masks have corroded into faces, to be able to read the human heart in a better light. The priest tries to stay awake and alert to our too easy fluencies, our avoidances, our bruises and our desires. To speak authentic words as a pastor is important. The language we turn to to help us get there is so often that of poetry. This is the language that distrusts the paraphrase, the quick clarity, the cliché and the avoidance of difficulty. It is the language that dispels illusions without leaving us disillusioned, helping people think in a language in which they never thought.

I'm from Shropshire originally, and there are a lot of sheep in Shropshire, and at the back of my grandmother's house I often see Tom who's a shepherd. And about three years ago I saw him in the field carrying a real shepherd's crook. So I joked with him that my boss the bishop had one of those too. And I asked him if he really used it to reach out and hook naughty sheep with and haul them in. No, he said. The best use for this is to stick it down firmly into the ground so that I can hold on to it so tight that I become still enough that the sheep learn to trust me. I have been desperate to preach at the consecration of a bishop ever since! But it's an image for any pastor in their community. How can I find that rooted place to centre myself, to keep me still in a turning world, that I can somehow be trustworthy, authentic, plausible to those I am among? When the poet Michael Longley was asked where his poetry came from, and he replied that if he knew where poems came from he'd go and live there, he implied that poetry has the potential to encounter a strange place that somehow feels homelike. The reader of poetry is a kind of pilgrim, setting out, setting forth to the unknown.

Wallace Stevens, a poet I'm drawn to more and more, once said that we ought to like poems as children like the snow.[125] And that air, the stark, clear, striking, warm-chill of poetry where we can see our own breath, as it were, and immerse ourselves in a world reimagined, a truancy from the prosaic and the surface, is why many a priest reaches for the pen or opens the book of poems. Like Celan's image of poetry as 'a message in a bottle'[126] or Graves' notion of it as 'stored magic',[127] poetry promises more of you at the end than at the beginning. This nearness to what matters, as human and as poet and priest, is exactly the quality so admired in David Scott. And when poetry mesmerizes time and captures, not imprisons, reality's nearness in the poem, life's immensities become so intimate and life's intimacies become so immense. In David's poem 'John Keats', he writes, 'He leaves whole bits / of life completely satisfied in words.' It is the poet's work to find the words from which we can't retreat.

The novelist Nicola Barker, winner of this year's Goldsmith's Prize, was asked recently what she made of religion. 'I'm interested in the spirit, the soul, and in suffering and transcendence,' she replied:

> I'm interested in paradox. It's my thing. I think people are full of contradictions. It's partially to do with the division between the conscious and the unconscious mind. We are mysterious beings, a mystery to ourselves, often. We are full of hypocrisies but are psychologically resistant to accepting this ... I can see a strong demarcation between pleasure

and joy. One is fleeting, the other is infinite. Sometimes I'm at my most happy while doing without. Desire can often be the enemy – though I rarely say no to a dark chocolate digestive.[128]

Ah yes, I was once a naughty student who said to my theology lecturer – 'for all your doctrinal headaches, take paradox'. But now I see what he was pointing to in both life and belief. The priest's and the poet's nearness to human complexity and chaos, to secrets and the things that we know but as yet have no words for, brings them close. Perhaps one of my favourite poems by David is his 'Written in Juice of Lemon':

Written in Juice of Lemon

Some poems I write in ink
and they get written with a lot
of furrowing of the brow, and often miss
but some I write in juice of lemon
quickly in my heart
and hope that one day someone's
warmth will iron the secrets into poems
with effortless art.[129]

Ironing the secrets into hearts means that the priest is concerned with the nearness of our language, wanting words that are not just learned but felt. This is not an easy time for words. To begin with we are living at a time when we are spending money we don't have on things we don't want in order to impress people we don't like. And so consumerism makes words seductive rather than truthful as they lure us towards our wallets. Technology for all its brilliance now also gives us too many words, we trip over them as they come at us from every direction, and the danger is that our care for words decreases as they proliferate. Listen to them all on the TV debates, social media, opinion columns: the first person to draw a breath today is declared the listener. The danger is that words become cheapened, as disposable as anything else.

And then there are our political leaders who, in many parts of the world, now campaign in graffiti and govern in tweets. At the moment the way words are being used by some powerful leaders, with continual talk of 'individuals' rather than 'people', of 'losers', 'swarms' and 'sad' failures, all makes a world where we see ourselves as competitors not citizens, consumers not communities. It leads to a world in which if you are not at the table you are probably on the menu. Nations at the end of the day are largely the stories they feed themselves and if fed lies they will, in time, suffer the consequences. Words become flesh. If words are used cynically, cheaply and as ammunition, if they are not respected as carriers of truth and meaning, then it quickly leads to human beings not being respected either. Note how similar those two words are – devil and drivel. And the same ears that listen to politicians, salespeople and news commentators are listening to the person who is trying to point to the rumour of God, to a sense that ultimately reality is trustworthy. Sadly the language with which we do this can reflect the superficiality or clinical vocabularies of the newsroom or the boardroom, the Church at the moment often sounding as simply offering you the choice between ignorance on fire or intelligence on ice.

This is another reason why priests often become poets. Because as well as being often local to a community, among people in their devotion and dereliction, reverence and rebellion, they are also, like it or not, ambassadors for an institution, an establishment and organization called the Church. Some do not find this a comfortable role. It's my experience that at the moment many people, especially younger people, realizing that there is something of a wisdom deficit in the world, are actually often very serious about religion, spirituality and the search as to whether reality might be worthy of faith and why that might be. But these same people do not find the Church to be a part of their spiritual adventure. In fact, the irony is that spiritually serious people today often find the Church to be too secular, too much like that from which they are trying to escape – cautious, compromised, politicized, discriminatory, or at best the bland leading the bland.

Now to imagine that its clergy are immune from feeling such things would be naive. Many clergy long for more poetry in their church. They long for a reclaiming of mystery, of beauty, of the humane. They know that at the evening of life we will be judged on our love not our systematic theology. They long for a humbler Church, more concerned to be kind than to be right. They – and why don't I show myself and say properly 'we' – we long for a Church that imaginatively commits itself to the God who is not an object of our knowledge but the cause of our wonder. This means accepting, as poetry does, that some things are far too important to be literalistic about – love and God for instance – and that therefore any fundamentalism is to Christianity what paint by numbers is to art. Such priests understand their religion as poetry plus not science minus. Church, for us, is a school where we try and relate a bit better to what is true, to ourselves, to each other, to God. It is not the ecclesiastical equivalent of the Sealed Knot,[130] dressing up on a Sunday morning to re-enact a former world. It is not the organizational equivalent of the character in the *Goon Show* sketch who always knew what time it was because someone once wrote it down for him on a piece of paper. It is a community trying to settle around a fountain from which wisdom emerges with patience and prayer, where we accept we are given just enough to look for God but never enough to fully find God, for desire is the pulse of faith; if that dies so does the relationship. What we long for most must elude us. Such a priest it is, I think, found here in David's poem 'A Priest at Prayer', which always reminds me of George Herbert's poem 'Prayer':

A Priest at Prayer

> From prayer to prayer involves
> a dwindling, a way of being
> that accounts for weariness, a regular
> drawing in and letting out of breath;
> the planting of a word and its forgetting,
> a close examination of what is there
> until it isn't, a candle flame beating air,
> love meeting Love before the house wakes up;
> space body-shaped, time vacated,
> the passive tense, a waiting to receive,
> out-of-bounds of what is right
> or wrong, subject to being surprised
> by God on briefest sight.[131]

One of the tests of faith as opposed to bad religion is whether it stops you ignoring things. Faith is most fully itself and life-giving when it opens your eyes and uncovers for you a world larger than you thought. The test of faith is how much more it lets you see and how much it stops you denying, resisting or ignoring aspects of what is real. Poetry has the same testing criteria. Poetry and faith are both disciplines of attentiveness.

My last reason as to why a priest might be drawn to poetry is that it is the language that most feels like a soul-language. And clergy, as they go about their work in churches and chapels, are indeed local poets in residence because poetry is their native language if only we can see it.

If I said to you now 'Here is the News' you would probably sit up and expect to hear the facts of the day, events that have occurred and some commentary on them. But if instead I said 'Once upon a time' you would probably be equally expectant for truth but you'd tune in differently and be ready to receive it in a different form, story, where meaning is communicated without summarizing it. Now, when you walk into a church or a place of worship, how do you tune in your ears? Have

EPILOGUE

you got your newsroom ears on? Have you walked into a Google temple of facts on tap? Or have you walked into a poem? You see, to walk in with expectations of the one and to get the other might mean you miss something very important. It might even mean you think the whole thing implausible. Category errors like this cause a lot of frustration in the brain and heart. Now just in case you think this is all a bit Radio 4, a little too 'I wondered lonely as a canon', let's just remember the ancient traditions of the great world faiths and the place poetry has in the heart of each.

The earliest sacred texts of Hinduism, the Vedas, are in effect thousands of poems, then the Upanishads and the Bhagavad Gita or Song of God, composed in verse. In China, the classic Tao Te Ching was written poetically in the sixth century BC, the opening verse referring to the 'gate to all mystery'. Then the Hebrew Bible, full of poetic exploration: the psalms, the noble language of Job, the imagery of the Song of Songs, the riddles of the Proverbs. And the prophets warning people what they've turned into, doing it through intense imagery and metaphor. It's a message today's Church needs to be reminded of, that prophets always call us to a proper vision with poetic hope and never with prosaic plans. I'll come back to the Gospels in a second, but let's jump now to the Qur'an, where God is the poetic author of a text so beautiful that Muslims developed particular chant styles for reciting it. Listen to its much-repeated line that has become the key statement of Islam's shahadah or confession of faith: 'There is no god but God', in the Arabic transliterated as 'la ilaha illa Allah'; repeating the double consonant il between the open a vowels gives it rhythm and emphasis to translate into your life. In these spiritual traditions truth is expressed through poetry for the faithful. Poetry isn't a better way of saying truth, rather truth is found in poetic form.

The Christian Gospels are not so obviously poetic until you study them closely. You then see the artistry of each of the four writers, or evangelists, as well as the persistently figurative preaching of Jesus himself. Jesus often left people wondering, it says in the gospel, what on earth he meant and yet being intrigued and drawn by his parabolic language that hovered rather than came into land. At the end of his poetic tales it said, 'If you have the ears to hear, then hear.' Might that be, have you tuned in right? This is not the news, you see. This is the good news – and language has gone into a state of emergency to help us get to the kingdom. From the moment the music starts in a service you sing a poem called a hymn, you recite a poem called a psalm, you pray prayers of metaphors, similes, allusions. A priest in her church is a person immersed, living, in a poem. No wonder poetry feels natural.

If I were to try and get to the heart of my belief as a Christian, I would say that belief is that God has given everyone here a great gift. It is your being. And we are all asked to give a gift back in return – our becoming, who we become in our lives. Put it another way: God loves us just as we are but God loves us so much God doesn't want us to stay like that. Therefore we need a language in our faith that is not so much about information as about formation, a language that helps us become. We need, and the stories of the poet Christ are this, a language that doesn't set out to answer all our questions so much as questions all our answers. We need a language that enlarges the heart, the mind, the humane and our understanding of the divine. Poetry is often hard. But that is because difficulty is important. Life is hard. Belief is hard. Difficulties there are important. Both poetry and true spirituality (not listening to whale music during a massage but the serious business of assaulting the ego) know that only difficulty can change us. It's the only way, apart from love, that our full stops can be turned into commas.

Just a final note about language: religious types easily slip into thinking language imitates or reproduces reality, what I say just is. Actually the poets remind us that language doesn't do this. Language re-presents reality. They allow us to see that language may be truthful even when it is not descriptive in the strict sense. We can claim to be speaking truthfully about our realities without trying to imitate them. For the poet, the use of language permits us to celebrate the fact that there will always be much more to discover than what we think we see. And that is why poets and people of faith have a conversation to pursue. As R. S. Thomas told us, poetry 'is that which arrives at the intellect by way of the heart'.[132]

Let me finish. I'm here to pay tribute to David Scott. I'm here to thank him for a life's work of nearness, of being an ambassador of humanity to the divine and a carrier of sacred perceptions into the human. I'm here to thank him for his faith, that assured reticence that took upon it the mystery of things as if he were God's spy. His is a poetry of receptive insight. I'm here to honour the poet who wrote that 'sometimes we can walk in Eden', the poet who is able to see the longing in a life, like that of St Teresa in his poem, a longing for 'more of the wounds of love and for the darts / that score the heart'.[133] And when I read David's work on faith and God I'm always reminded of the Manley Hopkins lines, 'I greet Him the days I meet Him and bless when I understand'.[134]

My guess is that there are people here now who would call themselves believers in God in one shape or another. Others here will not believe in God and others will not be sure one way or the other. Quite a few may sympathize with Graham Greene when he said, 'The trouble is I don't quite believe my unbelief.' And some will, like Julian Barnes, want to say, 'I don't believe in God but I do miss him.' And maybe most of us are a mixture of all the above. And my other guess is that for all this range of commitments, this daily landscape we live in of questioning and positioning, there is something most of us do feel drawn to – to cherish words, to celebrate their sacramentality, their ability to form us and so the world we make. People of faith and poets must both, together, do all in our power to ensure words remain fresh, true and honest. The person of faith believes that God is in this world as poetry is in the poem. The poet believes that reality is so excessive that only poetry can touch those intimate immensities and its immense intimacies, that a poem's work sends ripples out towards our shores, shifting the sands and stones for a purer truth. Both believe that if human beings have a soul-language, then this is it and that the poet's work is so vital that – should it be lost – the soul and maybe the world itself would be endangered.

I want to end with a poem by David, which he wrote in memory of another priest and lover of poetry, Donald Allchin, whose work greatly influenced many of us who carry on the exploration of faith and poem.

Give them some poetry
(*i.m. Donald Allchin*)

1

When first we met I saw a lightness off the ground in him;
the air of outside, high up, the world all sides of us,
had space to breathe the meeting into life.
A meeting that would last both in and out of time,
and all this as I saw it. It may quite well
be fixed inaccurately, but the height and the space
at the first, is sure. He in a cassock. I not.
He just back from America; I coming to the end
of school. I liken it now to other meetings,
other heights, grander and more biblical,
keen not to miss the precedents, and the connections:
Mt Alverna, say, or wherever light takes over from the dark.

2

Of the world he was not; born somehow
to have that extra inch or two which left him in the air.
So many ideas that others could organise,
which they did, and happily, on the whole.
He liked his spirituality corporate;
serving solitaries, he was not one himself.

EPILOGUE

3

Our common thread was Merton,
that English-American-Nowhereboy. Donald,
returning from Kentucky met the monk
the day that Martin Luther King died,
which left a generation seething, grieving.
I with a volume of some early Merton poems
newly spread with gravy from reading them
at meals and a term away from A-Levels.
From America, Donald wrote about an emptiness
of saints, and of a space unfilled by holiness.

4

Through all the years he came by saints and scholars;
scholars and writers and poets; and religious and hermits,
and poets: and rarely by children, but once he came by Lucy
in her cot, whose heart was not yet strong, and he prayed
and I saw him unusually paternal, and now she bikes up
mountains, and down again, in Wales.

5

And then came Wales for him, and how fresh it looked
upon the page away from English tightness.
He was forever inviting us to 'do Wales',
and got the words from Merton: 'Let's do Wales,' said Merton,
Donald did Wales avidly: so many poets, so many saints,
so many friends. Bardsey, in its distance, in its beauty,
a metaphor for death, for passing from one realm
to another. The journey had begun.

6

The handwriting turned frail.
The phone call said he was enjoying Traherne.
I said,
I was about to conduct a retreat.
He said:
'Give them some poetry.'[135]

Well, David, you have given us some poetry. You really have. And we hope you know, within you and around you, always, the gratitude, admiration and deep affection for that poetry and for you – truly, a priest and a poet.

Bibliography

Ronald Blythe, Penelope Lively, Richard Marsh, David Scott and A. N. Wilson, *Ink and the Spirit*, Canterbury Press, 2000.
Paddy Bushe (ed.), *Voices at the World's Edge: Irish Poets on Skellig Michael*, Dedalus Press, 2010.
Church Hymnal, Oxford University Press, 2000.
Roger Deakin, *Waterlog*, Vintage, 2000.
W. H. Gardner, *Poems and Prose of Gerard Manley Hopkins*, Penguin Books, 1953.
Gwendolen Greene (ed.), *Letters from Baron von Hügel to a Neice*, J. M. Dent & Sons Ltd, 1928.
Philip Larkin, *The Complete Poems*, Faber & Faber, 2012.
David Scott, *An Anglo-Saxon Passion*, SPCK, 1999.
David Scott, *Beyond the Drift: New & Selected Poems*, Bloodaxe Books, 2014.
David Scott, *Lancelot Andrewes: The Private Prayers*, SPCK, 2002.
David Scott, *The Mind of Christ*, Continuum, 2007.
David Scott, *Moments of Prayer*, SPCK, 1997.
David Scott, *Piecing Together*, Bloodaxe Books, 2005.
David Scott, *Playing for England*, Bloodaxe Books, 1989.
David Scott, *A Quiet Gathering*, Bloodaxe Books, 1984.
David Scott, *Sacred Tongues: The Golden Age of Spiritual Writing*, SPCK, 2001.
David Scott, *Selected Poems*, Bloodaxe Books, 1998.
R. S. Thomas, *Collected Later Poems 1988–2000*, Bloodaxe Books, 2004.

David Scott's published works listed chronologically

1984 A Quiet Gathering.
1989 Playing for England.
1989 How does it Feel? And Other Poems.
1997 Moments of Prayer.
1997 Building Common Faith.
1998 Selected Poems.
1999 An Anglo-Saxon Passion.
2000 Ink and the Spirit, with Ronald Blythe, Penelope Lively, Richard Marsh and A. N. Wilson.
2001 Sacred Tongues: The Golden Age of Spiritual Writing.
2002 Lancelot Andrewes: The Private Prayers.
2005 Piecing Together.
2007 The Mind of Christ.
2014 Beyond the Drift: New & Selected Poems.

Plays produced for the National Youth Music Theatre

Captain Stirrick, first performed 1980.
The Leaving of Liverpool, 1981.
Bendigo Boswell, first performed 1983, BBC TV.
The Powder Monkeys, 1984.
Jack Spratt VC, first performed 1985, Edinburgh Fringe First, 1985.
Les Petits Rats, first performed 1989, Sadler's Wells.
also
The Dream of the Rood, 1993, a sacred music drama commissioned by St Albans Abbey for their Twelfth Century Celebrations.

Endnotes

1. Unpublished poem, used by permission of Miggy Scott.
2. David Scott, 1989, 'The Surplice', in *Playing for England*, Bloodaxe Books.
3. *Beyond the Drift*, p. 233.
4. *Piecing Together*, p. 18, from the poem 'Meeting St John of the Cross'.
5. *Playing for England*, p. 32, from the poem 'A Walk with St Teresa of Avila'.
6. *Selected Poems*, p. 132, from the poem 'A Nun on the Platform'.
7. *Piecing Together*, p. 44, from the poem 'Pablo Casals Plays to the Wall'.
8. These include 'For John Ball' (*A Quiet Gathering*, p. 15), 'For Martin' (*A Quiet Gathering*, p. 28), 'For Brother Jonathan' (*A Quiet Gathering*, p. 70), 'For Norman Nicholson' (*Playing for England*, p. 51), 'For Pete Laver' (*Piecing Together*, p. 22), 'For Frances Horovitz' (*Selected Poems*, p. 126), 'With Miggy at Skelwith Force' (*Piecing Together*, p. 27), 'On Not Knowing R. S. Thomas' (*Beyond the Drift*, p. 196), 'Canon Fenton, Theologian' (*Beyond the Drift*, p. 228), 'Miss Taylor, Church Organist' (*Beyond the Drift*, p. 229), 'Together: An Elegy' (*Beyond the Drift*, p. 231).
9. *Sacred Tongues*, p. 16.
10. *Sacred Tongues*, pp. 32–3.
11. *Playing for England*, p. 23.
12. *The Mind of Christ*, p. 17.
13. *The Mind of Christ*, p. 17.
14. *Beyond the Drift*, p. 238.
15. *Piecing Together*, p. 40.
16. *Piecing Together*, p. 41.
17. *Playing for England*, p. 29.
18. *Playing for England*, p. 23.
19. *A Quiet Gathering*, pp. 58–9.

20 *Playing for England*, pp. 36–9.
21 *A Quiet Gathering*, p. 66.
22 *A Quiet Gathering*, p. 38.
23 *Piecing Together*, p. 36.
24 *Selected Poems*, p. 137.
25 *Selected Poems*, p. 139.
26 *Playing for England*, p. 15.
27 *The Mind of Christ*, p. 65.
28 *The Mind of Christ*, p. 65.
29 *The Mind of Christ*, p. 65.
30 *The Mind of Christ*, p. 65.
31 *The Mind of Christ*, p. 65.
32 *The Mind of Christ*, p. 66.
33 *Selected Poems*, p. 146.
34 *Selected Poems*, p. 151.
35 *The Mind of Christ*, p. 66.
36 *Selected Poems*, p. 153.
37 *Selected Poems*, p. 154.
38 *Selected Poems*, p. 155.
39 *Selected Poems*, p. 157.
40 *Selected Poems*, p. 158.
41 *Beyond the Drift*, p. 193, from the poem 'In its substance is but air …'.
42 *Beyond the Drift*, p. 197.
43 *Beyond the Drift*, p. 199, from the poem 'Evening Light'.
44 *Beyond the Drift*, p. 245.
45 *Piecing Together*, p. 39.
46 *An Anglo-Saxon Passion*, p. x.
47 *An Anglo-Saxon Passion*, p. xviii.
48 *An Anglo-Saxon Passion*, p. xix.
49 *An Anglo-Saxon Passion*, pp. xx and xxi.
50 *Sacred Tongues*, p. 103.
51 *An Anglo-Saxon Passion*, p. xxxi.
52 *Playing for England*, pp. 26, 27.
53 *Beyond the Drift*, p. 234.
54 *Beyond the Drift*, p. 235.
55 *The Mind of Christ*, p. 138; emphasis original.
56 The letters were edited by Gwendolen Greene and published in 1928.
57 *The Mind of Christ*, p. 140.
58 *The Mind of Christ*, p. 142.
59 *Church Times*, 6 April 2023.
60 *Church Times*, 6 April 2023, p. 21, col. 3.

ENDNOTES

61 *Church Times*, 6 April 2023, p. 21, col. 3.
62 *Church Times*, 6 April 2023, p. 21, col. 3.
63 *Beyond the Drift*, p. 180.
64 *Beyond the Drift*, p. 181.
65 *Piecing Together*, p. 23.
66 *Piecing Together*, p. 23; the poem is the full text of 'The Church of the Holy Sepulchre, Jerusalem'.
67 *Piecing Together*, p. 24.
68 *Piecing Together*, p. 24.
69 *Piecing Together*, p. 25.
70 *Piecing Together*, p. 48.
71 *Piecing Together*, p. 50.
72 *The Mind of Christ*, pp. 147, 148.
73 *The Mind of Christ*, p. 148.
74 *Selected Poems*, p. 138.
75 *Church Times*, 6 April 2023, p. 21, col. 3.
76 *Piecing Together*, p. 59.
77 *Beyond the Drift*, p. 209.
78 *Piecing Together*, p. 63.
79 *The Mind of Christ*, p. 152.
80 *The Mind of Christ*, p. 152.
81 *Piecing Together*, pp. 60–2.
82 *The Mind of Christ*, p. 152.
83 *A Quiet Gathering*, p. 79.
84 *Piecing Together*, p. 57.
85 *Playing for England*, p. 9.
86 *Piecing Together*, p. 64.
87 *The Mind of Christ*, p. 153.
88 *Moments of Prayer*, p. 26.
89 *Moments of Prayer*, p. 27.
90 *Playing for England*, p. 54.
91 *A Quiet Gathering*, p. 28.
92 Carrowkeel to Portsalon is a journey from north Donegal to just south of Sligo, a distance of about 100 miles that can take three hours to drive! Plenty of time to see the scenery. The slopes of Murren, 227m high, would be seen looking east from the coastal road.
93 *The Mind of Christ*, p. 154.
94 *Beyond the Drift*, p. 248.
95 *Piecing Together*, p. 55.
96 *A Quiet Gathering*, p. 43.
97 'Poplar and Ash', from *A Quiet Gathering*, pp. 23, 24.
98 'Dusk and Lough Derryduff', from *A Quiet Gathering*, p. 32.

99   *A Quiet Gathering*, p. 46.
100 *A Quiet Gathering*, pp. 47–3.
101 *A Quiet Gathering*, p. 54.
102 *Playing for England*, p. 16.
103 *Playing for England*, p. 44.
104 *Piecing Together*, p. 10.
105 *Piecing Together*, p. 20.
106 *Piecing Together*, p. 31.
107 'Gertrude Jekyll's Lindisfarne Garden', in *Piecing Together*, p. 28. NB: 'Gertrude Jekyll's Lindisfarne Garden' on page 206 of *Beyond the Drift* is an entirely different poem.
108 *Selected Poems*, p. 115.
109 *Selected Poems*, p. 118.
110 *Selected Poems*, p. 123.
111 *The Natural History and Antiquities of Selborne* was first published in 1789.
112 *Selected Poems*, p. 133.
113 *Selected Poems*, p. 134.
114 *Selected Poems*, p. 139.
115 *Selected Poems*, p. 140.
116 *Selected Poems*, p. 159.
117 *Beyond the Drift*, p. 230.
118 *Beyond the Drift*, p. 240.
119 *Beyond the Drift*, pp. 241–4.
120 *Beyond the Drift*, p. 246.
121 *Beyond the Drift*, p. 247.
122 Philip Larkin, *The Complete Poems*, Faber & Faber, 2012, p. 35.
123 Frances Havergal referred to this hymn as her 'consecration hymn'. It was published in 1874, and in her own collection of 1878, *Loyal Responses*, it is preceded with a quotation from the Oblation Prayer from the Service of Holy Communion in the 1662 Book of Common Prayer: 'Here we offer and present unto Thee, O Lord, ourselves, our souls and bodies, to be a reasonable, holy and lively sacrifice unto Thee.' *Companion to the Church Hymnal*, Columba Press, 2005, p. 783.
124 According to Donne: 'It is not the depth, nor the wit, nor the eloquence of the Preacher that pierces us, but his nearenesse; that hee speaks to my conscience, as though he had been behinde the hangings when I sinned, and as though he had read the book of the day of Judgement already' (*Sermons*, 3.5.142).
125 The quotation runs: 'People should like poetry the way a child likes snow, and they would if poets wrote it.' Wallace Stevens.
126 The full quotation is: 'A poem, as a manifestation of language

and thus essentially dialogue, can be a message in a bottle, sent out in the – not always greatly hopeful – belief that somewhere and sometime it could wash up on land, on heartland perhaps. Poems in this sense too are under way: they are making toward something.' Paul Celan, quoted in Josh Felstiner, *Paul Celan: Poet, Survivor, Jew*, Yale University Press, p. 115.

127 'True poetic practice implies a mind so miraculously attuned and illuminated that it can form words, by a chain of more-than-coincidences, into a living entity – a poem that goes about on its own (for centuries after the author's death, perhaps) affecting readers with its stored magic.' Robert Graves, *The White Goddess*, Faber & Faber, 1999.

128 From an interview by India Bourk with Nicola Barker, 2017, *The New Statesman*, 8 November 2017.

129 *Piecing Together*, p. 64.

130 The Sealed Knot is a re-enactment society that performs historical scenes, especially from battles of the English Civil War. Members dress as soldiers of the period and usually perform where the original battles took place.

131 *Selected Poems*, p. 158.

132 R. S. Thomas, 2004, 'Don't ask me ...', *Collected Later Poems*, p. 355.

133 'A Walk with St Teresa of Avila', from *Playing for England*, p. 32.

134 Gerard Manley Hopkins, 1953, 'The Wreck of the Deutschland', *Poems and Prose of Gerard Manley Hopkins*, Penguin Books, p. 14.

135 *Beyond the Drift*, p. 200.

Index of Poems

Numbers in regular font are pages in this book, and those in italics are in *Beyond the Drift* (except where indicated as *Piecing Together* and *Selected Poems*)

Abbey Ruins 22, 70, *134*
A Boat on Iona Bay 45, *163*
A Botticelli Nativity 21–2, *132*
A David Jones Annunciation 14–15, 18, *173*
A David Jones Nativity 17–18, *174*
Allhallows Church 70, *240*
A Long Way from Bread 21, 22
An Afternoon Walk 59, *248*
A Nun on the Platform 3, *127*
A Peculiar Clarity 45, *178*
A Postcard from Lake Trasimene 70, *134*
A Priest at the Crematorium 26, *145*
A Priest at the Door 26–27, *146*
A Priest at Prayer 27–30, 79–80, *149*
A Priest in a Bookshop 27, *148*

A Priest in a New Parish 25, *144*
A Priest with the Bible 25, *142*
A Quaker Sitting 24, *138*
Ash 63, 26
Astley Church 71, *247*
Autumn in Wivelrod 61–2 (in *Piecing Together*, *55*)
A Walk with St Teresa of Avila 3, 83, *75*

Between 69, *128*
Border Ballad 64, *41*
Botanical Gardens 20, *50*
Bowes Churchyard, Early Morning 70, *230*

Caedmon's Song 67, *159*
Canon Fenton, Theologian 9–10, 55, *228*
Castlerigg Songs 22, 62
Churchyard under Snow 18, 74
Cleaning the Shoes 68, *114*

95

Crucifixion, 1926 37, 234
Curlew 64, 41
Cycling Holiday 62, 35

David Livingstone on the eve of discovering the Victoria Falls 19, 45
Driving home from Basingstoke Crematorium 30, 198
Dusk 69 (in *Selected Poems*, 134)
Dusk and Lough Derryduff 63, 31

Early Communion 21, 34
Easter Poem (I) 36–7, 52, 186
Easter Poem (II) 36–7, 52, 187
Easter Poem (III) 36–7, 52–3, 187
Evening Light 30, 199
Excerpts from the Passion 36, 72
Eyes 21, 170

Flanking Sheep in Mosedale 64, 40
Flower Rota 54, 59
For Brother Jonathan 6, 52
For Francis Horovitz 8, 122
For John Ball 5–6, 20
For Martin 6, 58, 28
For Norman Nicholson 7, 93
For Pete Laver 7, 160

Gertrude Jekyll's Lindisfarne Garden 68 (in *Piecing Together*, 28)
Give them some poetry 84–6, 200
Good Friday and the Magnolia Tree 37, 235

Heart on Pilgrimage 44, 161
Herdwick 64, 40

Ibn Abbad woke early 67, 166
In its substance is but air ... 29–30, 193

John Keats 76, 116
Just a Line 57–8, 95

Kirkwall Auction Mart 62, 17
Knowing too much 30, 199

Mea Shearim, Jerusalem 45, 162
Meeting St John of the Cross 2, 157
Michelangelo's Rondanini Pietà 48, 185
Miss Taylor, Church Organist 10, 229
Mist 64, 39
My Bike 70, 150

Nine Lessons and Carols; A Theological View 31, 245

INDEX OF POEMS

Old English Household Life by Gertrude Jekyll, 1925 63–4, *38*
On Not Knowing, R. S. Thomas 9, *196*

Pablo Casals plays to the wall 3, *175*
Poplar 63, *25*

Qumran, Cave no. 4 45, *162*

Rain 64, *39*
Reading Party 9, 18–19, *70*
Reflections on Craigie Aitchinson's Paintings 4 33, 36, *172*
Resurrection 51, *188*
Retirement 30, *197*
Ruskin's *Sketches from Nature* 64, *42*

Scattering Ashes 53, *56*
Selborne, some 29th of Junes 68–9, *119*
Skellig Michael: A Pilgrimage 42–4, *180*
St Herbert's Isle, Derwentwater 49–50, *209*

The Annunciation of the Blessed Virgin Mary 1, *233*

The Awe that Falls on Language 14, *238*
The Church of the Holy Sepulchre, Jerusalem 44–5, *161*
The Closure of the Cold Research Institute 65–6, *87*
The Deserted Barracks 68, *111*
The Friends' Meeting Room 45, *177*
The Funeral 53–5, *183*
The Lanercost Poems 70–1, *241*
The Presbytery Cellar 19, *46*
The Ruthwell Cross 47, *133*
This Meadow, a Soul 66–7, *153*
Tintern Abbey 71, *246*
Together: An Elegy 12–13, *231*

Village Organist 19–20, *79*

With Miggy at Skelwith Force 8, *164*
Written in Juice of Lemon 55, 77, *188*